"*Breathing Stone: Living Small in a Southwest Village* immerses you in the magic of the New Mexico desert. Mammals, birds, reptiles, insects, and plants spring to life through the sharp, observant eye of Betsy James. This book is an unexpected gem sparkling in sunlight."

—**Judith Schiess Avila**, author of
*Code Talker: The First and Only Memoir by One
of the Original Navajo Code Talkers of WWII*

"A must-have for anyone who has ever lived in the desert Southwest or who dreams to. A perfect combination of prose, poetry, and line drawings. If you've never lived in a village in the Southwest, this book will entice you. If you have, it will feel like coming home."

—**Dr. K. Kitts**,
NASA Primary Investigator and Science Team Member

"Transcendentalist poet and iconoclast Henry David Thoreau wrote in the 1850s that 'The question is not what you look at, but what you see.' He also commented that he had 'traveled a good deal in Concord.' In this slim volume, poet and painter Betsy James has taken the New Englander at his word, only what she has seen is in New Mexico and she has traveled a good deal in the ancient villa of Placitas at the foot of the Sandia Mountains. She bested Thoreau, in my opinion, with a keener eye and a broader sensitivity to her environment.... This book is a genuine addition to New Mexico literature."

—**Don Bullis**, historian,
New Mexico Centennial Author

"Sojourn in the natural historic beauty of Placitas
Walk its ancient trails
Listen to wind in the tall grass
Glimpse an owl in solemn flight
Find deep quiet in an old adobe on the old mountain
Escape to another time"

—**Martha Liebert**, author of
Bernalillo: Between the River & a Hard Place

"Betsy James's sensitive and poetic reflections and observations of four years living in a New Mexican village make you feel as if you were accompanying her through all seasons."

—**David Grant Noble**, author of
In the Places of the Spirits and
*Ancient Ruins and Rock Art of the Southwest:
an Archaeological Guide*

Breathing Stone

Other works by Betsy James

Roadsouls
Listening at the Gate
Dark Heart
Long Night Dance
Rattler (forthcoming)

Breathing Stone

Living Small in a Southwest Village

Placitas, New Mexico, in the Nineties

Betsy James

Casa Urraca Press

A B I Q U I Ú

Cover artwork, "Ghost Roads," by Betsy James.
Author photograph by Jeanette Williams.
Interior designed and set by Megan Kornreich.
Set in Museo Slab and Mostra Nuova.

26 25 24 23   1 2 3 4 5 6 7

First edition

ISBN 978-1-956375-15-2

CASA URRACA PRESS

an imprint of Casa Urraca, Ltd.
PO Box 1119
Abiquiú, New Mexico 87510
casaurracapress.com

Our Solar System

Nearly forty-five years in this place
where air moves,
water falls,
light glitters with dust.
What I have learned here:
to turn my face toward the buzz of a hummingbird,
to shut my eyes against sand.
All the lessons of the universe begin
with what presses against the body.

Placitas, New Mexico
February 1992–November 1995

The rural village of San Antonio de Padua de las Placitas, New Mexico, is in the throes of becoming a bedroom community for Albuquerque, some twenty-four miles to the south.

The village's deepest roots are Indigenous. It lies at the northern end of the Sandia Mountains, which were rich with deer, elk, and bear. Springs and llanos supported wild plants like piñon, rice grass, and prickly pear, and later corn, beans, and squash. Then came Spanish conquistadores and settlers; kidnapped genízaros; a flood of European miners, hippies, suburbanites. Waves of culture washed the little village. They still do.

For almost four years in the early nineties I rented part of an old adobe near the village center. I had worked for years with cultures very like those that had shaped Placitas—in Mexico, Albuquerque, Zuni Pueblo. I was a writer, an artist, and a backcountry hiker. I decided I would regard each day as I would a hike off-trail in new country: I would *notice*. I would give this place my best mortal attention, and then record what I could.

This is the result.

Year One

February

There is an infant burial under the floor of the room. They say.

I was told:

Old Placitas had no church. It was a visita, a village the priest visited sporadically. The closest church was a dozen miles away, down Las Huertas creek in San Felipe Pueblo. If you died in Placitas, they say, you were tied to a ladder—as bier—and carried down the arroyo to San Felipe for proper burial.

Unless you were an infant. Then you went straight to paradise, an angelito. You might be buried under the "canal"—the downspout of the roof—to be baptized by the rain from heaven. This was especially true if the canal was that of the chapel where the visiting priest performed his services. The room where I sleep stands where the downspout of such a chapel poured its rain.

They say.

There *is* a baby buried under the floor of this room. That is the true thing.

> The task
> is to find out
> what the baby is.

A pickup passes on the road, the dog in the back woofs enormously as it is borne along: doggie Doppler. Horses pass, clop-clop. The street should be dirt. There's a sense of time blown away like smoke, another century happening beyond the adobe wall.

Night coagulates out of the wet air.

A fire in the fireplace. The room smells of cedar, so sweet. Southwest generations and eons of woodsmoke husky in the back of the nose; the fluttering of flames. One side of the face hot and tight, the other cool.

Night in Placitas

At the stillest moment
of the night:
seven pistol shots
and their echoes.

A crowding host of insights, of new thoughts. As though the thoughts had been here in this old house already and were eager to have a new consciousness to enter and inhabit.

The room is full of spirits: drafts, eddies of wind. As if the air were crowded with moving entities. Not malicious—just the ghosts of everyone who has lived in this place, their human histories. The pistol shots are part of it.

A good place. The huge geraniums that make a forest in the west windows are healthy because the house is full of spirits. I read the Spanish poet Antonio Machado aloud, loud. The room is sonorous with the echoes of human voices.

The house needs a name. Hawks in the Cornfield House? Because as I write there is one.

Time blown away. From me, too: time is passing, better pay attention to the curve of the red road beside the field of yellow grass. The western horizon is white, Cabezón is cloaked in snow and hung above the yellow-brown-russet valley. Over the Rio Grande a blanket of fog lays arms of mist along the acequias.

On the village street a Great Dane, a tan one, came barking and licked my hand with his warm, soft tongue.

Cold, brilliant sun warms the old walls. The birds are happy and sexy, the geraniums raving red.

Placitas, New Mexico. We lean toward spring.

March

All night the wind blew. I woke and listened, watching the last embers of the fire. Come morning the distant mesas were purple and yellow and red, mottled with storm.

Sunlight across the page picks out the grain of the paper. The wall heater clanks and roars softly. The tea is hot.

On my walk this morning there was a bird like a fat robin with a speckled breast, a black napkin at its throat. Maybe it had red under its wings. What was it? As I turned toward home, the fragmentary call of a coyote, wavery and high.

Ditch-cleaning is done. The acequias are running, a smell of wet earth pervades the village.

April

Near six, not yet evening. I've watered everything I can reach with the hose. The wind blows. I'm on the patio in the weathered old chair, sun on the paper. The apple tree above the arroyo is white as a bride and full, full of bees.

Around here, sunlight is a loud word.

May

Total silence. Meaning: wind. Birds. A dog yelping far off.

Summer comes to an old, still house and its ghosts.

There is so much life packed into and under this place that it *is* life. Thick, fat, strong-as-a-weed-root summer pushes outward here, green and spiny and rank.

A break from weeding. Chapped hands, finger cut on a broken beer bottle. I've pulled one zillion spiky mega-dandelions, eight zillion left. I'll have to make death forays every couple of days. They're a jungle inhabited by fat ladybugs and darkling beetles.

Maybe I won't pull them.

Puebloan shrines, even the important ones, are minimalist. A pile of rocks. Noninterference: not wanting to stand out as different from nature. This is true in Zuni, from the little I know. Is it true in Placitas, where Puebloans and their ancestors have lived for thousands of years?

Night. Heavy rain. The air is cold, spicy, dark. Two crickets in the courtyard creak. Only the screen door between me and the night.

Far off, a neighbor is hammering something.

Wind at night. Hoarse voice that speaks and speaks.

Last day of May. The wind sighs afternoon on the patio. This place is too beautiful—just the ordinary beauty of the world.

Basics

Walked all day on stone.
Came home, drove the Datsun down
to town and bought a chicken
already roasted.
It was hot. It made that old car
smell like love fulfilled.

House on a hill, it looks far off to slanting mesas and mountains of granite and snow. House of adobe and wood, of limestone with crinoids and fossil corals. Constant wind and moving air: house on the mountain's flank that catches every storm.

Road sounds float up to it.

Crooked doors and windows, steps up and steps down, odd corners. Wide, worn floorboards, salvaged windows.

Four hummingbird feeders.

Scraps of juniper bark and sawn sections of dead poplar are stacked by the door: firewood. There's a worn coconut mat for muddy feet. Colored smooth stones from a prehistoric river, gathered and spread on the patio stones. Hikers' finds: horseshoe, geode, rusty enamel cup. Well-used garden tools. Miles of faded green garden hose. An overturned wheelbarrow, old buckets turned upside down, a chile seedling in a red clay pot.

In the cottonwood a tiny warbler shouts.

Old-fashioned rosebushes—eglantine, wild rose—and spindly new ones, splashed with mud. Grappling over the wall, a Don

Juan rose so red it's black. A rambler clambers furiously above the septic tank: the Septic Rose.

An acequia.

Dill in a forest. Thyme, rosemary, sedum scramble among the rocks, zinnia yearns toward the sun. Old lilac trees make caves for children to play under: shiny heads, shiny leaves. There's a plastic mother duck lying on her side in the lilac foliage; puppies had eaten the plastic ducklings.

A frondy tamarisk. A pear tree, an apricot, an old gnarled apple. A mulberry tree, a gooseberry bush. Portulaca thriving and fat. Everything snarled together with bindweed.

The land steps away into the arroyo. In the dry wind the cottonwoods and poplars show the undersides of their leaves.

June

Max DeLara keeps the house from sliding into the arroyo.

He's a lean, handsome man in his seventies, Spanish and French Huguenot he says, handy with a hammer or a mason's hawk. He grew up here. As a teen he gathered oral history for the WPA, and he is full of stories. As I sat in the shade of the mulberry, Max plastered a crack in the east wall and talked.

What I knew already:

The earliest Spanish settlement, in the late 1700s, was San José de las Huertas, a fortified land grant village on Las Huertas Creek. Until about 1868, anywhere outside the Rio Grande Valley wasn't a healthy place to settle, if you liked living. The Navajo—properly the Diné, though Placitas histories use "Navajo"—raided from the west, other nomadic Natives from the east. Above Placitas there's an Apache Canyon, though it seems to me those raiders were most likely Comanche or Kiowa. As the raids abated, Hispanic settlers could at last live in villages that were scattered, rather than consolidated in one armed and fortified plaza. Hence placitas, "little plazas."

Max says:

There's an old pueblo next to the land grant spring. That would be the Spanish land grant: seventeenth or eighteenth century.

Where is the spring? There's a salt lick south of here, "behind the hill." Which hill?

At eighteen, Max's grandfather, José Librado Gurulé, who lived well into his nineties, went by wagon with his father to Kansas to buy salt. When he pulled a frying pan out of the wagon in the dark it triggered a loaded shotgun and blew off his left arm. He cut off the mangled remains himself.

"Manco" in Spanish means "one-armed."

Years later, Gurulé was attacked by a bear. A grizzly? The last recorded grizzly in New Mexico was shot in 1931, well south of here. Gurulé's friend—a sheepherder, owner of the only gun they had between them—ran away in terror. Max's one-armed grandfather wrestled the bear, wielding only a stubby knife. He held onto the bear's tongue, says Max. (I hear the grandfather's storytelling voice, see the grandchildren listening transfixed.) His friend recovered his wits, ran back, and shot it. His grandfather's back was ridged with claw scars, says Max, his shoulders clotted with bite marks.

Max says the man who lived in this house long ago was so strong that even when he was old he would hike into the mountains and lie in wait on a ledge above a deer trail, drop a rock on a deer's head to stun it, then drag and wrestle the living deer down the mountain and kill it at home.

Max was born in 1920. A different world.

There are still lions in the hills. At dusk neighbors have seen them, going back to the mountain.

Creeping Suburbia

Max says
when he was a kid
in the twenties, the mountain lions
came down the arroyo and crossed
to the Jemez Mountains,
forty miles northwest.

I think of them at night,
sleek cats
supple as water,
slipping down the creek
through the leafy dusk.
They can't cross the valley now,
says Max. There's the freeway.

Where do they go, then?
Where does water go
when you dam it?
Do I live on a mountain
that is slowly, invisibly
deepening in lions?

In the beginning heat of a summer Saturday, the high-ceilinged main room of the house is dark and still and full of pasts. Breakfast is happening on the front patio and the kitchen is cheerful with frying bacon, but that room keeps its history to itself. Under the shadowy tall ceiling, taxidermied animal heads gaze: pronghorn, deer, mountain goat, and a peccary with its nasty snarl.

The owner bought them in thrift stores. The room was grandiose, he said; it needed them.

It lacks a moose.

I walked up the village street to the San Antonio de las Huertas Land Grant Spring, off Dome Valley road en route to the old hippie enclave in Gringo Gulch. In forty minutes, two cars passed. Max says that years ago, when the village enlarged the reservoir, the backhoes dug up pottery and arrowheads and skulls.

The ragged fence that marked the enclosure was draggled and down. There was an unreadable sign. I stepped over the wire.

The wind blew. Tracks ran here and there through a dense, moving greenery of weeds and river cottonwoods. I pressed through a copse of waving willow fifteen feet high, the withies a handspan apart and well leafed.

Coyote paths ran through it. The wind blew the crown of leaves overhead. An eerie place, a labyrinth. I thought of bums, irate landowners, dogs. Maybe even—cf. Max's grandfather—a mountain lion or a bear.

Beyond it, the spring itself was a round hole surrounded by yellow stonework. Maybe six feet across, with a sandy floor roiled by underwater spurts and geysers. Clear, clear water. From the spring a channel ran, and from the channel an acequia branched into the undergrowth in a rush of working water. The rest of the overflow went to a pond, a frog haven of scum and cattails shadowed by rustling cottonwoods, reflecting bits of sky.

I crept back through the willows and around the nose of the pond. The ground was felted with willow catkins and cottonwood leaves, but here and there were sherds, flints, a broken obsidian knife, earth-stained broken bones that were probably deer bones but, from their color, might as easily have been human burials dug out and dumped by the backhoes.

Downhill in the arroyo a huge cottonwood had a tire swing and a treehouse. Well-made crosspieces climbed the trunk. Deep in jungle, a wild child place.

The knocking boom, musical as a drum, of ditch water through a galvanized pipe.

Soft explosion of doves from a telephone wire, clap of wings.

Spiderwebs woven over the irrigation ditch are full of cottonwood fluff. In the Spanish of Albuquerque these cottony seeds are "tatones," but I can't find a related word anywhere. Not even in Cobos's *A Dictionary of New Mexico and Southern Colorado Spanish,* nor in my last resort, Macazaga's *Vocabulario Esencial Mexicano,* which pins down so many Aztec words that wormed their way here via Hispanic settlers. Does tatón then come from a Puebloan language?

Literally it would mean "big tato." What's a tato?

... A neighbor corrects me: it's "tetones," big tits. Because the seed pods, before they burst and spread their fluff, look like nipples.

Oh.

Outside my bedroom window an orb spider has woven a web. One of the guylines is four feet long.

Blue-green buffalo gourd gropes and twines, beginning the orange blossoms that smell like a bad school cafeteria.

The rains have come.
  After rain the world is *pungent.* Wet hay. And petrichor—the Zuni word for it is *ołdi,* with the barred, unvoiced ł that is the same as Welsh LL.
  The mulberry leaves hang so low it's hard to see the mesa.
  There are four fat apricots, low on the tree.

Ay Dios. The county in its wisdom has painted a fluorescent orange double stripe down the village lane. The lane is so narrow that this leaves traffic six feet on either side of the stripe.

Muddy sowbugs trundle through the garden dirt like trilobites on the floor of an ancient sea.

Evening. The imperceptible fade of the sky from orange to blue, the orange tint bleeding down behind the mesas until there is only paleness left. Venus appears. Then the Big Dipper. Nighthawks on

narrow wings tumble in the air: the slope falls away beneath them until they are high above the roofs of the village below, the black pointed poplars, the generous round dark cottonwoods. *Beent. Beent.* Their nasal cry is never in the same place as the bird: the bird drops its call and flies on.

> The plangent twang
> of a nighthawk
> narrow in the air
> Westward,
> the cool mesas step away

Windy house. The air is never still. I wake in the night with air rushing past. It has traveled hundreds of miles over desert and llano, over night-feeding rabbits and mice and owls, over red spires of stone, over the volcanic hulk of Cabezón all alone on its prairie. When it reaches this patio it surges in the dark mulberry leaves.

From Here

> To the northwest,
> the mesa's still, flat,
> sleeping slopes seem
> to lean a little,
> wearing at their edges,
> crumbling into the river.
> Because I have walked there, I know
> those edges are black basalt
> blocks the size of boxcars,
> pecked with petroglyphs
> by dead hands. But from here
> the mesa looks like what it is:
> sand
> crumbling into the river.

The crowned apricot has borne six fruit.

July

We never *arrive*. To arrive is not our calling. We're process. Verbs.

In the patio, mating crane flies fly joined together at the tail.

Something is eating the corn. First there's a circular chawed place, then wind blows the stalk over.

When anyone is watering around the house, the sound echoes and rings in the old pipes.

As I tossed out mop water, something rustled purposefully in the dry leaves: a fat foraging lizard eight inches long. It raised its head and looked at me with a bright eye, then went busily back to work. Usually lizards are stretched at full gallop, but this one curved its almost-chubby body until the skin of its side wrinkled in tucks.

Night. North over Tonque Arroyo all is dark purple cloud. Lightning fizzes down.

Heat: white, confusing, dull. The corn has shriveled.

Many grasshoppers.

On the top of a cerro to the east is what looks very much like a Pueblo shrine: an insignificant cluster of stones, time-sunk in the ground. From it rise three tufts of grass. It overlooks the distant green cottonwoods that mark the spring.

Old Adobe in Summer

If I had refrigerated air
I would be cooler,
more efficient,
and I would not know
what the oshá knows,
sun-beaten,
silent,
potent at the root.

Flying in from out of state I saw Placitas from the air. Green lines of trees trace the acequias. On the plains to the north, the groove of Tonque Arroyo and the faint site of old Tonque Pueblo.

Home again. Evening storm light on the ripening apples.

The heart of this place is deeper and older than anyone who has lived here. Max is slapping yet another skin of stucco on the house.

Snakes *shed* their skins.

Here the human
turns to earth.
Corn has been grown here
for a thousand years.

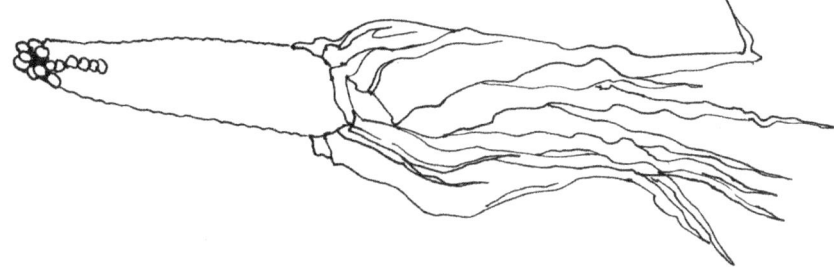

Grasshoppers froth out of the arroyo in thousands; they leap away at any movement.

Battered wooden doors with black hasps. Pots with animal faces. Indian rugs, black and red; a gray rug with a woven labyrinth.

Stove with a bent stovepipe. Round fireplace, a round chimney that rises from it in stone steps. (Stone steps to nowhere went up the wall above the fireplace at my grandmother's house, a childhood mystery.) Nichos cut right into the adobe wall.

The animal heads on the wall are expressionless except for the snarling peccary.

All is still, as though no one has lived here for a thousand years.

How the wind blows in this room! It's like standing on the prow of a ship, a figurehead breasting the huge air.

A friend and I hiked to the land grant spring. There is a lime kiln dug into an arroyo bank: circular, walled at the lower end, burned red, a pile of smashed limestone above. Early nineteenth century? But the early nineteenth century was still the time of Navajo and Comanche raids, terribly dangerous for settlers. The earliest Spanish village wasn't by the spring, but was a fortified settlement down on Las Huertas Creek.

Max says the kiln was in use during his childhood.

Just off the village road, en route to the spring and above the old fields, this geologist's daughter found a tiny old malachite working: spoil-hole and tip.

Three scrub jays are catching grasshoppers in the weeds. Their startled, straight-up jumps match those of the hoppers. They are a dusky, dusty blue.

In Balance

I am home,
and for this moment I am right
as the gray scrub jay in the patio
who shouts up night.

Morning thunder climbs the ridge.

Yesterday Max put a new door into the kitchen. He chopped out the old adobe with a hatchet and found an old window, its header made of aspen logs.

He says he learned to read from the magazine pages his mother used for wallpaper behind the wood stove, the coziest place in the house.

The broad bamboo-grass leaves are beaded with rain. In the arroyo the chassis of a red convertible is overgrown with stink squash.

Max is still plastering. His homemade scaffolding is gray and beaten, round-cornered, nailed and re-nailed, many holes.

He says on the ridge behind his folks' house there was a flint-knapping place where he found arrowheads.

It poured. I walked anyway. Crawling in the middle of the village street was a lunk-headed ugly slow salamander, six inches long, with little starry paws like a mole's and such a muddy greenish yellow it was hard to find its eyes.

I picked it up and looked for a ditch to put it in. At first it was passive. Then it began to squirm, slowly and firmly: slippery, tense body, flapping tail. I crawled through a fence and dropped it into the grotto where water that soaks down from the ditch has carved a tiny cave with a pond, rooty and full of the sound of dripping. Salamander paradise.

The black stink bug that sticks its butt in the air, the Darkling beetle, in New Mexico argot is "perrodo," from Spanish "pedorro," "farter."

Max still plastering. After his latest mention of "a girl I was dating"—in the forties or so—I said, "Max, was there any girl in New Mexico you didn't date?" He said, "The population was much smaller then."

Today, there's so much iodine in the village drinking water it makes my nose wrinkle.

Now and then, a single note from a bird in the mulberry tree.

Thirty mourning doves with creaking wings burst from the Indian rice grass and sat on the phone lines. They have such tiny heads.

A violent afternoon storm. The air was white with rain, the wind howled and whipped the poplars. A foot-deep gully appeared in the dirt road, and the arroyo ran with slipping brown water. The grass is so deep there that you could barely see the water twinkle.

The roof leaked.

Then the sun came out bright. The neighbors stood around looking at the gash in the road, the stones fanned out across the pavement.

Monsoon

Storms in the body.
Storms in the heart.
All gates down.
Great waters, great winds.
Who could stand?
Who could stand?

Wackwacka in the green cottonwood, a big woodpecker with a speckled back.

This morning, out strolling on the hill I like to climb was a fat brown ant almost half an inch long.

A cat got into the main house this morning before light. I heard yowls, then the *koosh!* of a smashed clay pot.

At the land grant spring two striped potsherds had washed down into the road gravel.

Found the season's first green acorn fallen on the road.

August

Rufous hummingbird at the feeder. A little Napoleon.

Somebody down the hill has a new electric guitar and can play two notes. Has been playing them for two hours.

On a hot summer night there are two kinds of crickets: one sounds like jingle bells, the other like a sewing machine.

Outside my window Max is polishing stucco with a mason's float, silent and alone. I am writing at my desk, silent and alone. Probably I wear a look of intent focus identical to his.

This world is ordinary and beautiful. I wonder at humans' apparent craving for the violent and bizarre.

Morning sunlight. Still. The sun rises late. First hint of cold.

In the bathtub four pillbugs are walking round and round and round and round.

This afternoon a friend explained to me, step by step and in detail, how to rid a house of ghosts.

I don't want to rid this house of ghosts.

Hiked the Crest Trail from Tunnel Springs. Hot and dry.

Spotted, caught, and rubbed the bellies of no fewer than eight horned toads. Their undersides had the typical Sandia Mountain coloring, a bright carnelian; one was a deep lemon yellow. They lay in my hand totally mesmerized, and at first didn't move even when I set them back on their feet.

I will be grateful to this place every day of my life.

Last night, the moonlight white as plaster. This morning, a praying mantis. Always the mean little hummingbirds. Bending heavy grass heads on the narrow crooked red road, potsherds boiling out of the bank below the spring: one black-on-gray fragment had been edge-ground into a gaming piece with eight stripes.

The air is full of water, the sloping angled mesas misty and dim.

A neighbor child, about four, told me solemnly, "I found a ring in the ground, and it wasn't even dirty. A silver ring, and it was treasure."

At the TOT market in Bernalillo a lanky three-year-old in his mother's shopping cart squeaked at me. I squeaked back. We squeaked in unison. I said, "Why are you squeaking, Mister Mouse?"

His mother snapped, "Because I told him he couldn't bark."

At Coronado National Monument, the Kuaua murals: Kwelele, younger son of the Sun and god of heat. They say. Is that correct, or just what some anthropologist thinks? Out of Kwelele's hand comes what looks like fire.

Dusk. The sky is Prussian blue and Payne's gray. In total silence, lightning over the distant Jemez: bright strikes, thunderbloom. No sound. Again. Again.

We saw a praying mantis *catch a hummingbird.*

The mantis was poised on the feeder. The bird approached. Backed off. Approached. Speaking as the mantis, my brother said, "If I take this home to Martha she'll forgive me for everything!"

The mantis grabbed the hummer by the head.

The bird shrieked, we leapt up shouting, the mantis lost its grip and the bird flew off, squeaking wildly. The mantis fell to the ground.

I carried it away from the feeder, down among the corn. Normally I'd herd a mantis onto my hand; this one I picked up on a stick.

Under the bay windows a Jerusalem cricket, apparently made of translucent amber plastic, was trying diligently to dig its way out through the brick floor. Its big-headedness made it almost appealing, for an insect. I caught it under a beer glass and carried it out to the compost heap.

Clear, cool autumn light. In the valley it is still summer. Here on the mountain, fall has come.

Back from a hike in the Sandias. Still thinking about a ridge on the mountain face, four thousand feet up, that looked out over the smoggy loud dirty spawning city. About the silence under those trees.

September

Hiking with a friend out by Cabezón I cracked a stone and found an ammonite. Sudden racket-roar; over the mesa rim, close, came three Hueys like flying black forts: hovering, dark, their blades flickering like hummingbird wings. They drove west and vanished over the next mesa.

When we got home I put the ammonite in water so I could scrub it with a toothbrush, a bit superfluous since until two that afternoon it had been encased in stone for 130 million years.

This morning an orb spider had built a web right across the road, maybe twenty feet wide. Did it hope to catch a Mitsubishi?

Evening. Faintest glow of red on the cerro, the one I think has a Puebloan shrine on its crest. As far as I know it's nameless. I'll name it:

Cerro del Santuario? Too grandiose. I don't know a word in Spanish to imply that subtle pile of rocks.

Cerro de la Hierofania.

Cerro Posa: "posar" means "to perch," like a hawk. A "posa" is local for a descanso—the place, often marked by a pile of rocks, where pallbearers set the coffin down to rest.

Posa also means "butt"—something else you'd rest on after you'd set down a coffin or, in nineteenth-century Placitas, a ladder with a corpse tied to it.

Cerro de Mañana, because I walk there in the morning.

Distant and blue, the mountains where I have walked. The sky is full of high, streaky cloud.

A katydid, lime green in the evening light. A clumsy creature, it flies briefly and crash-lands, is good mostly for holding a pose, like the verdigris bronze dinosaurs in front of the Museum of Natural History. It moves like a city bus, needs a row of lights along its side.

By moonlight the apples are black globes against a silver sky.

Sunflowers wide-eyed in headlight glare.

The arroyo.

Human beings can't resist throwing things away. That is, inventing an edge or boundary beyond which things are termed "away," gone, not real anymore. Our primitive and self-serving minds hope *out of sight* means *no longer a problem*.

The arroyo below the house is full of things people have tried to throw away. It's an uncivilized world, an Other. Old T-bones, bottles, rusted bedsprings and crumpled iron whatnot, hundred-year-old potsherds, sun-purpled glass. A wilderness of human trash.

A juniper grows out of the arroyo's eroding wall; nameless trees and bushes thrive in its wetter, jungly depth. There's a cholla forest, a bosque of wild cherry trees, tall grass where the grasshoppers breed. In the arroyo a stream of wildness runs through the village—a river of bears, coyotes, lions, and rejected human darkness.

Secret, hidden, forbidden. Another country, invisible from the windows of the house.

Children know this.

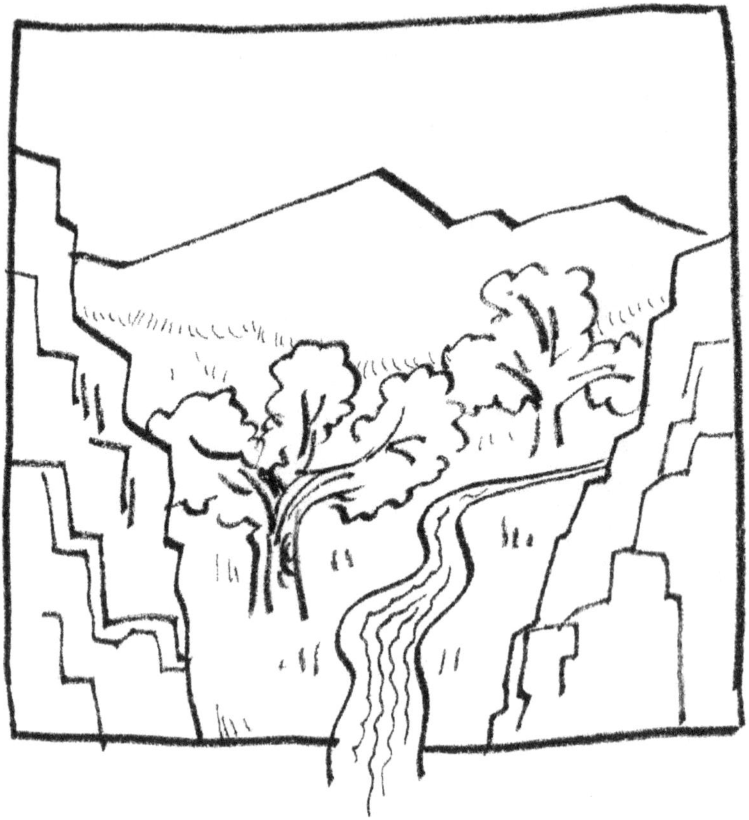

An autumn wind blows, blustery and cool and big. A slab of banded red-and-yellow sandstone holds the essential stillness of the desert, the big real world in which we are grains of sand.

When the Spanish came, the Puebloan settlement under the cottonwoods and willows of the land grant spring was already a ruin. It was a ruin in the thirteenth century, asleep on its sunny, quiet hill. Laughter and talk and the barking of dogs had gone from it, its people shifted elsewhere, one small human cycle finished centuries before these hills saw a European face.

On Not Exploiting These Ancestors:
Advice for Immigrants

Gather your own loves round you.
Do not ape the native. Toss down
among this worn adobe and this grass
words in your own tongue.

Respect these ghosts. Do not adore them.
Let the sage and desert weed
set down roots, grow up seed, until the mound
is soft, hiding the sherds
as new hair hides a scar.
Only now and then a stone, like a tear,
comes tumbling out of the arroyo-side.

Offer European wine.
Not flutes. Not drums. Not feathers.
You are not needed here.
These souls make their peace without you.
Love them. Let them be.
You have blood to shed in your own time,
you have your own
suppers to cook, tears to weep,
your own body to lay down.

The dead are fertile. Be alive.
The living feed the peaceful dead.

I went down into the arroyo, a small animal among the wild morning glories that bind the rusty trash, to break and scatter a bead necklace for the ending year. For dying and dissolution and fear, the slow darkening of the light.

Love of the half-seen. Not *wanting* to know in hard-and-fast, finished ways. The fallen pile of bricks that might have been the corner of a house ruin, but on a closer look turns out to be an old barbecue: how much more interesting, how many more possibilities, if once it had been a house!

To a child, anything built before their birth is prehistoric. A derelict Texaco station is as archetypal as Stonehenge.

The sweet whistling across the arroyo turns out to come from the white-haired caretaker of the Catholic bell chapel—Misión San Antonio de Padua—as he waters his roses. The roses are pink; they bloom furiously for him because he whistles. Around their roots he builds waffle gardens that he fills with water as clear as his whistling. His name is Arsenio Durán.

Fallen apples lie under the trees in red drifts. Just up the road from the church lives a family accused of beating their baby to death.

The stillness of objects. It is a timelessness that is all mortal: if I could watch long enough I'd see that their stillness is dissolution and reformation.

Sunlight through a window, moved by moving leaves.

> If I didn't sit silent in the dark,
> what would I miss?
> Heartbeat of least moth,
> breath of mouse
> in apricot shadow,
> faint sigh
> of grass leaning to winter sleep
> or April resurrection?
> This am I: chronicler
> of the footfall of the fly,
> scribe to the hiss of light,
> notary to the leaf
> as it mumbles at the window
> for the trillionth time
> and, this time,
> falls.

October

Flocks of birds fly crying from the mountains to the cerro. Why?

This night, the first winter wind. It whines at a different window than does the summer wind. I am cozied down in a comforter in the dark.

North of Cerro de Mañana, coyotes howl in the wrinkled brown hills. When they bark they are dogs, but when they sing in their high, unstable voices they are the voice of wildness itself.
    The wind is cold. The grasses wintry, white, dry.

This morning, when I ambled frumpily into the bathroom in the half dark, something big, black, and hairy strolled across the tiles.
    I thought: *Rat!* and bailed out the bathroom door. Black-and-hairy dove just as fast in the opposite direction and huddled behind the toilet.
    It was a *huge* tarantula. I caught it in a pickle jar. It was covered in dusty brown fur with worn patches, like a well-loved teddy bear. I didn't like the look of its fangs, though I don't think it bites; people let our local tarantulas walk up their arms. I hope it has no local, as in this room, friends or relatives.

I'd forgotten that in the fall the males are out hunting for a mate. The females can live twenty-five years, I've heard, but the rambling males wear out in a year or two. Surely male tarantulas have been stumping across this bit of earth for thousands if not millions of years—long before someone built a room over an infant burial, where baptismal rainwater fell from the canales of an old chapel.

A pretty sentiment. Be that as it may, this guy will live out his days in a terrarium in the classroom of a neighbor's eight-year-old.

The leaves of the apricot are yellow, and the thorny New Mexico locusts are turning. The mulberry is still green, but now and then a bundle of leaves falls on the flagstone with a clack.

The cornstalks have dried. Grasshoppers are dead or slow, crickets silent, birds few. Mom called; she had watched a documentary that said the birds are dying, there are so many fewer than there used to be.

Distressed, I went for a walk in the well-water-cool, glass-clear autumn light, and the earth here comforted me. In the street I picked up a very pregnant mantis, her wings crisped by frost. I carried her to the red bend in the road and set her on a bush to finish what she was up to, birthing or dying. On the Dome Valley road a lizard ran sparkling off.

At the land grant spring there was sunlight on the water; water skaters and wind and reeds and willows were all shining. Four pairs of mating dragonflies perched in the willows, their long tails doubled over.

Beautiful world, survive us.

Near the mission church, almost obscured, is a circle of stone that a neighbor said was once a village well. Also the foundations of the old sala, the dance hall. In the twentieth century before the advent of radio, dance bands traveled from one small community to another, bringing the music and sexy wild hope we all need, in some form, to keep going.

All I have to go on is local myth. It's good to find out the truth, but it's also good to delight in the color and pathos and hope that humans turn the truth into.

Weathering out of the edge of the arroyo right below my windows was an Archaic mano: a grinding stone used to crush native seeds like Indian rice grass. It's a hand-size, oval granite cobble with a flat plane worn on either side.

I knew they must have been here, the early ones, the Archaic pre-Puebloans. They built pit houses, dug into the earth for warmth. They had no pottery or bows and arrows yet but made baskets and hunted with atlatls, spear-throwers whose length extended and intensified the arm strength of the hunter.

Of course they would be here. There's water, the land grant spring. A good place to live. The mano has been out of use two thousand years or so, but still perfect to crush garlic.

In the PBS special *Surviving Columbus,* Rina Swentzell, of Santa Clara Pueblo, said, "People who walk on the land leave their sweat and leave their breath, so that place never forgets us. And if we go back to that place, we can partake of those people through their sweat and their breath."

As many miles as I've hiked in New Mexico, folks around here are partaking of *my* sweat and breath.

The fuzzy desert moon hangs in the west,
soft as a peach.
All the water in the world
could not call me from this sand and stone.

Folks up the road killed two rattlesnakes. Another was dead on the road to town. Like tarantulas, they wander in the fall, hunting for mates.

I don't know the names of the old gods of this place, but I suspect the pantheon of the woman who used that mano included rattlesnakes.

Early morning: a bird whose call is like tapping two agates together.
Later: a bird whose whistle is one sweet, plain note.

Half the mulberry leaves are brilliant, green-tinged yellow. Maybe they've been so for days, and I've been too sad to notice them. Now I do.

At the first blue-gray light the valley is full of mist. It looks like Seattle, and I'm so glad it's not.
The hills are dark, furry with misty pine.

November

There was a great horned owl in the cottonwood, big as a German shepherd, so big it looked mammalian. It scratched itself with one claw and stared. Precisely at the moment when I thought, subliminally, *dusk*, it stretched wings and floated out over the valley.

Long wings. Maybe a five-foot wingspan?

An owl's ears are on its face, near its eyes.

First snow. The heater purrs. Distances are blurred, the stemmy weeds fringed with white. There are still a few green trees, a few leaves on the lilac bush. A late, warm fall.

Silence. Snow falling in empty space.

Snow. Big, kissing flakes. Somewhere the rusty screech of geese. A flock of small birds calls, blustering off into the falling white.

Yellow leaves leave the mulberry. The instant of decision is soundless. A faint click and tap as the leaf touches others in its fall, and then it is on the ground, motionless, as though nothing had changed.

Morning. Windless. The mulberry leaves shower down like rain.

The rest of the mulberry leaves fell all in one day. Green, yellow, brown, a thick carpet waiting for wind.

A swelling moon tonight, still and clear.

Names of Placitas dogs, bestowed by myself because I don't know their real names but on my walks I like to talk to them:

Leo

The Meyers Boys, after a pair of childhood bullies

Stubby Boy, who has no tail

Old Dog

Huge Dog

Angeline the Barker

Creepy Dog

Tootsie

Pretty Eyes

Little Big Mouth

Wind Chime, tied permanently to a tree

Night. Soft, tapping rain on fallen leaves.

The cricket that stowed away when I brought in the geraniums creaks once. Is silent. Creaks.

Last night I woke to long rain on the roof. This morning is blustery, all mud, but there's snow on the mesas beyond the river. A winter look, those miles of snowy prairie. The Rio Grande wears a boa of fog.

The mulberry leaves, green and yellow just a week ago, are already a mat of brown jelly. The air is damp and brisk and sweet with rotting leaves.

Dry, ticking snow slants in on the wind. Juncos hop in the hen scratch, crying *Tsst! Tsst!*, their tails straight out like pot handles.

A cold, hard wind. The ice on red puddles in the upper road is smashed by passing wheels and freezes again, icebergs in a frozen sea.

There's still water in the acequias.

Rain in the night, snow in the morning. When I opened the door to throw grain to the juncos, the air was wet and sweet. Branches waved against the gray sky.

The juncos are smooth birds, impeccable, in silk slates and browns with kohled eyes and little executioners' hoods. They don't look like city birds. When they fly they show white on either side of their tails.

Backyard Physics

I think there's a compressor somewhere
with an air hose with which
the juncos inflate themselves
to a precise PSI.
We should find out how they do it.
It might be valuable technology,
pertinent to the ping pong ball.
But I'm doubtful about
industrial applications. Juncos
are so exquisite they're almost
theoretical,
sleek and busy as atoms,
perfect as the concept of a sphere.
I feel I should offer them something
refined, ethereal:
the wine of light, or
quarks in gossamer.
What they like, though, are
day-old doughnuts.
For these they bounce and dance
like—we all learned this—
molecules in hot water,
maintaining a low boil
till a roving cat ups the heat.
In a flash they change states:
as a body they
expand,
explode,
evaporate.

The woodpile is wet. Max moved it when he stuccoed the wall and I forgot to put it back under cover. The wind is full of soft snow that sparks on the cheek. Now and then the fireplace fire blusters in a downdraft. Poplar logs burn long. In the big, dark, soft, snowy night a hen cackles furiously, a sharp sound in all that softness.

Snow itself smells sweet.

Four or five inches of snow in the night. I woke to hills pink-white, sky blue-white. I've always liked thresholds, dusk and dawn. We love the half-seen because on it we can project our vague desires. But there's another love of twilight that's based on an openness to things in flux. Who knows where that white road leads, or what is hidden by that pink skin of snow?

The juncos pick at scratch, up to their chins like deep-powder skiers. I'll sweep for them and scatter more corn.

Waking on Sunday, Placitas

Wind cracks at the windows,
snow finer than dust
falls between me and the mountain.

The church bell bangs!
After the clang,
a humming in the air.

The snow is melting fast. Rivulets pour down the dirt street of Las Ciruelas. Not a chuckle of water but a hiss, almost a sizzle, as ice crystals rub on the sand.

… Here I interrupt to chase a spider off my arm. It can be a spider somewhere other than on me.

The cricket in the geraniums sings
as if it were summer.

December

Hiss of wind in the stiff brown cottonwood leaves that still cling to the trees around the land grant pond.

It's winter.

Colors are brown and white. Long underwear. Cold brick floors, cold toilet seat. Heater's clank and hush. I shrink from the walls; the adobe sucks up all heat. In an old Hispanic adobe the hearth fire would not go out all winter; perhaps the house walls stayed warm as a slept-in bed.

Birds tap at the window feeder. The dark comes soon.

"Storm warning. If you live outside the city, better get gone."

By the time I was halfway to Bernalillo the freeway had slowed to twenty-five. Snow iced and clotted on the wipers. I *crept* up the mountain. At the S-curves cars and trucks and trailers were in the ditch. The village road is steep at the Presbyterian church so I kept on, creeping up the highway to the far junction, crept back down, and rolled at last into the driveway under the cottonwood. Home.

Now the wind sucks at the house in the dark. I keep thinking I hear trucks passing but it is the wind, tugging and roaring at the mud walls. There were eighty-mile-an-hour winds in the village this afternoon. The post office door blew off. Now: blue darkness. Somewhere above the clouds the light has not quite gone; the faint bulk of Cerro de Mañana is pale against a paler sky.

A few distant lights shine as though through mist, but it's through blowing snow. It's dark in here, just a string of lights and two candles. *So beautiful.* I wonder where the juncos are. How does something so small stay warm in such a wind?

Morning.

The wind never stopped. The dry sharp flakes lie in drifts. I forced the door open, swept the porch, and laid out crumbs. Now thirty or forty fat juncos and sparrows squabble over buttered bread, all puffed up against the wind. They won't eat blue corn tortilla chips, even crushed; they don't seem to recognize them as food. I went out to walk but turned back. There was no way to keep ears warm against the blast off the mountain.

The sun, barely risen over the eastern ridge, blinked through a tear in the clouds and everything was silver, scoured by wind and dusted with ground-glass snow that smoked off roofs and chased itself down the street in rills. The world shone like an Advent calendar.

Winter Morning

Out there
the snow tears sideways.
Dark-eyed juncos
quarrel, the wind blows
down their collars,
up their pantaloons.
In here
the steam
rises almost straight
from the warm cup.

Bitter cold. This morning a fog packed everything like smoke, twigs and branches were rimed with frost. A white, lost world.

My hands are chapped. I've been trying to keep the heater of the main house on enough to keep the pipes from freezing. More snow is due.

A pewter day. Cerro de Mañana isn't red—the colors that show through the snow are the yellow of dry grasses and the dim green of frosty juniper.

In the leafless mulberry cling the remains of three bird nests.

The waning morning sickle moon is the same milky blue as the snow. A flock of mountain bluebirds chatters past, flashing their iridescent backs.

The slim white wolf-dog down the street is in estrus, red blood on her creamy flank.

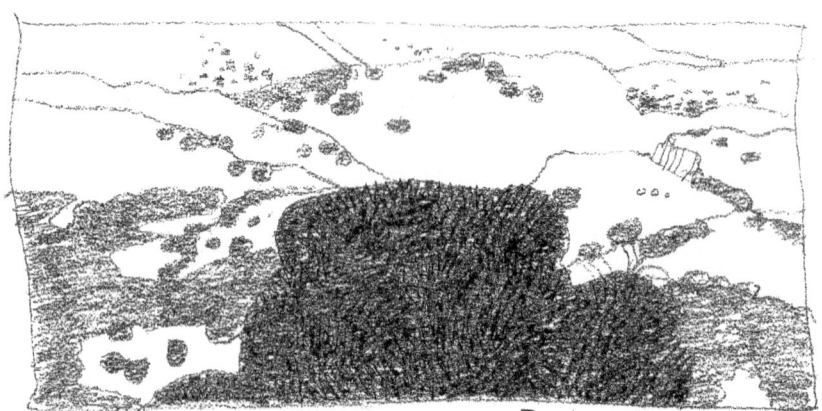

WHAT IS IN THE WORLD WITH THE PIÑON. PH 12-8.9 3

Quiet

This place deserves peace,
repays peace
with peace.
Be still.
Your whole childhood
lies under this age's noise.

January

Santo Domingo Pueblo, the animal dances. I stood by the plaza wall on cold feet and felt the drumbeat in my legs.

It's January. Where is all this dark wet coming from?

In my life I have shifted from beginnings to continuations, but the continuations have an endless supply of little beginnings in them.

I love the eroticism of beginnings.

Woke to rain, a patter hard on the windows and soft on the roof, the morning too dark even to be blue. Sounds of rushing water, the rain's walking feet. The roof leaks.

Morning walk: fingers of damp streak the houses' adobe walls like desert varnish. All colors are toward purple. A Northwest winter, indigo and inward. The bitter old man who farms up the way told me angrily that these heavy clouds are caused by people having water heaters.

Placitas has three cemeteries. The old Catholics and the newly-converted Presbyterians refused to be buried near each other, and there's an early land-grant cemetery, though I don't know where that is. The Catholic cemetery is next to the post office. There are many children's graves, mostly from the teens and twenties. They seem to be grouped at the east wall.

Some of the soft old sandstone gravestones were clearly carved by the same hand. Their sometimes-phonetic spelling makes me think about how straightforward Spanish is to decode, compared to the horrors of English. Even non-readers could sound out the words and understand what was being said.

A gilded evening of pink clouds and silver air, soft chinook winds. The hills are red with sunset. Then night comes, purple and blood.

From Placitas

Beyond the mountain
the city burns
like false dawn.
Here, only wind
with a few souls in it.
Black trees.

Something is moving.
We do not know what it is.
It does not care much who we are.

The wind has been blowing
for a long time.

I who write these words
am a colony of colonies
burning in wind.

In old Europe people were often named for their *places*. The Duke of Argyll would be simply "Argyll." My family has been four centuries in the so-called New World, more than a century in the West, yet my name is still entirely European.

New Mexico geology at a glance:
Cretaceous: 65 to 144 million years ago
Shallow seas that advanced and retreated.
Rivers and river deltas.
Big dinosaurs.
Jurassic: 144 to 208 million years ago
Aeolian (dry and windblown) deposits.
Middle-sized dinosaurs.
Triassic: 208 to 245 million years ago
Surface water deposits: braided streams.
Little dinosaurs.

Sandia Crest, though, is the Pennsylvanian, which was about 300 million years ago. That limestone, full of crinoids and fusulinids and horn coral, weathers out as boulders that roll down Las Huertas Creek.

I Ching Geology

"The dark element
opens when it moves
and closes when at rest.
The strictest reticence
is indicated here."

The twin-shelled brachiopod
opens,
claps itself backward
through the indigo deep
and closes.
In the Pennsylvanian shales
I find it, still closed:
three hundred million years
of strictest reticence.

I've been teaching writing workshops at Zuni Pueblo. The Zuni bless and thank by scattering white cornmeal with chips of turquoise ground into it. Around the old houses in Halona, the main village, the earth is speckled with turquoise.

For the Zuni, there are certain places along the Sandia Crest that are sacred. Mountains have such being that I would be surprised if that were not so. Once, hiking the Crest, we left the trail, walked to the limestone brink and looked west over the valley and the vastness beyond. My companion looked down at our feet. Said, "Oh."

There was a tiny grain of turquoise among the clifftop gravel. Somebody prayed there.

On a whim I went to Coronado National Monument, the ruins of Kuaua Pueblo. The water from the campground pumps is delicious.

I chatted with the ranger, who is from Santa Ana Pueblo. Because in Zuni the kachinas Kwelele and Shitsukya bring the new year's fire, I asked him about that many-horned being in the kiva murals who is identified as Kwelele, son of the Sun, god of heat.

He looked away. He said carefully that he was a Keresan speaker, the Kuaua people spoke Tiwa so he couldn't speculate on their religion or iconography. I understood that this meant, "It's not appropriate for me to talk about this."

I was ashamed. I should have known better. I apologized for asking.

Two redtail hawks flew up the river.

It's January, but sometime about last Friday I started to think: *Spring.* There's a softening, and odors. The trees around the land grant spring have been full of noisy birds. Last week I half noticed that; this morning I *noticed.* They are all robins. Twenty, thirty—calling and yelling and chirping and flirting.

In the city, a thousand feet lower, the daffodils are poking up their noses. Not here.

Year Two

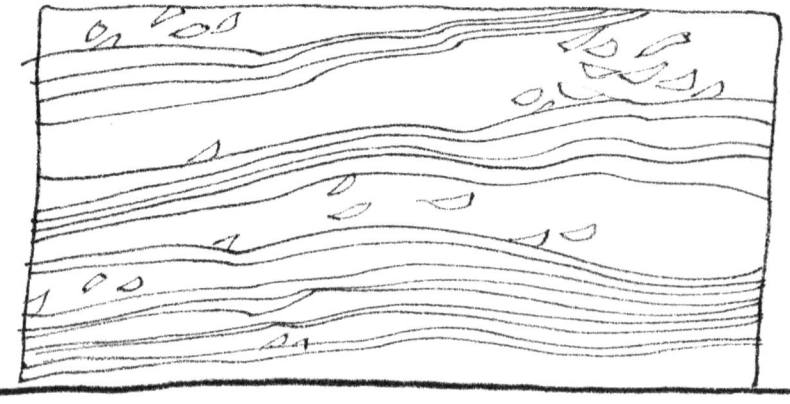

SOUND OF WIND IN LEAVES OUTSIDE WINDOWS BEHIND MY HEAD

February

Windy, gray. Stones frozen to the ground.

> Perhaps there is an instant
> when everything that has been dying
> is dead.
> Winter.
> Winter stays winter
> until something
> rises.

The air has a loosening in it. Big.

In the night a cold rain rattled the heater's tin chimney. This morning the valley is filled with mist, all the way up the arroyo to the empty chicken coops. Drops hang on each cold twig. The birds were here early, waiting for me to fill the feeder. The California towhee yells peremptory squeaks.

Spring is in the works. The robins were around all winter, but they weren't *shouting*. There's a pungent, spicy odor of leaves and earth. The rain brought out colors: yellow grass, red willow.

I keep looking for my daffodils. Not yet.

A cloudy-bright, blue-gray and red, racing windy morning. Not March, just motion. In the village there's much activity of the tree-trimming, fence-building kind.

Cabezón, the base of which I hiked around last Sunday, stands clear and dark and wears a beret of cloud.

Prowling in the arroyo this afternoon I found thick, clunky, historical potsherds, maybe made at Santa Ana Pueblo and at least a hundred years old. Got a swat of cholla spines in the leg.

When the church bell rings the white wolf-dog howls. She hears that vibrant after-hum.

Gray and snowy. In the patio a crowd of juncos argue over oatmeal.

After a snowfall the bend in the red road is white, with bright red puddles bleeding through.

In the nineteenth century the Navajo would come from the west, cross the Rio Grande at Angostura—"angostura" means "the narrow place"—and ride up Las Huertas Creek to raid the old fortified settlement. Did Apaches come from the east down Apache Canyon, or were those Comanches, which would make more sense? Farther south in the Rio Grande Valley, in the early nineteenth century, the Comanches practically owned the place. Did they hit communities this far north?

West of the present village there was a torreón, a tower from which to watch for raiders. A road is named for it. Max says its stones were long ago taken to build houses.

The white wolf-dog jumped her fence and went down among the new housing developments. A man thought she was a real wolf, and shot her.

There was a lot of mining in Placitas, says Max.

The mine below Cerro de Mañana was a coal mine, for local use only. Villagers would dig as deep as they could before the pit filled with water—they couldn't afford a pump—then abandon it and start a new one.

There was prospecting for many minerals, even gold and mercury. He says there are still many deep tunnels.

He spoke of the Treaty of Hidalgo as though it were yesterday. "It was *written down* that the land grant belonged to my grandfather, and that the grants were to be honored and not taxed. And they've taken the land, and taxed and taxed." When the land was in dispute the people were poor; the originally huge Spanish land grant was divided, and the white lawyers demanded a third of the land in payment.

Similarly, he said, in the early days when Placitas grew its own wheat and the growers took it to Bernalillo to be ground, the miller took every third bag as payment. For that reason old women still used the traditional grinding stones, mano y metate. The work crippled them and made their wrists and fingers swell.

I just heard the year's first thunder. No stories about Coyote or Rattlesnake until next winter.

Again the arroyo. Full of human trash: iridescent glass, broken bottles, potsherds. A road for dogs, cats, coyotes, mountain lions. Sometimes for people.

At the bottom, trees grow furiously, a thicket to lose yourself in. Varied bushes—what are their names?—make a hideout for birds. Tall grasses have been pushed flat by traveling water: the flood has passed, but the grass keeps the shape of its pressure.

Most of the arroyo is invisible from ground level. Those in the house rarely think about it. Beyond the rusty barbed wire at the edge it's a lawless world, where people shove their bad stuff, anything they don't want to look at, their bad side.

The arroyo belongs to no one, really. It's a no-man's land, a secret country of animals and water. On the hill next to it a neighbor woman said she saw "fairy lights."

The arroyo is much, much older than the house.

Canyon Wren

Like desert rain,
your cool note falls
from rock
to rock,
fading
before
it
hits
the
ground.

Hiking the road to Tecolote with a friend. We stepped over downed barbed wire and rusty heaps of tin cans from the fifties and headed up Las Huertas Creek.

There were tufts of cottontail fur from a recent coyote kill, the blood still pink. That one won't have bunnies this year.

We crossed the creek and sidehilled across the escarpment on the east side. Max was right that Placitas was a mining area. *There are open shafts.* One had a rusty headframe. One, with some cribbing still in place, was at least seventy-five feet deep—and open.

I'm a miner's daughter. Since childhood I've been warned away from open shafts. I remember tales of children who fell down them—stories that even now frighten me in my leg bones.

I have no idea who owns these mines. There were a couple of tumbled stone-and-adobe houses with halos of glass and old tin cans, a chipped white enamel washbasin.

We left the open holes and went back across the creek, to a ruin at the mouth of the draw. The scatter of long human occupation surrounded it: flakes, sherds and busted bottles, everything from a broken obsidian atlatl point—Armijo style, about four thousand years old—to a bit of glass that read MURINE.

There was a beautifully made well. Circular, built of blocks of red sandstone, the water surface maybe eight feet below ground level. Who knows how old? Also the remains of a wind pump whose iron pipe, about six inches across, still stuck out of the ground. I dropped a pebble in. Silence; then an eerie, resonating twang and splash as it hit water. Maybe thirty feet deep. As with the abandoned shafts, I imagine too easily an irredeemable fall into the dark.

The ruins of the stone house stood next to the totally-melted ruins of an even older adobe that crawled with cholla and tumbleweed. Judging by the sherd scatter, underneath those dwellings must lie the ruins of a pueblo, maybe even a pit house, with an Archaic and—who knows?—a Paleo campsite under all.

A nice place for a house is a nice place for a house.

Bobcat

In the gray limestone canyon,
I saw a bobcat!
A reddish-black bundle,
rabbit-shaped,
ran straight up the limestone cliff
like a house cat
up
a
telephone
pole.

March

The dogs I've been calling Pretty Eyes and Little Big Mouth have been joined by a brindled bitch with her spaying suture fresh on her shaved belly. She followed me happily halfway back to the village, so I turned around and walked her back home.

Blustery big winds. Eleven daffodils are above ground.

The house's big room is dusty with the ash of winter fires, chips of kindling scattered on the bricks. The big tin gas heater hisses, shuts off with a bang and clanks as it cools.

All the windows are salvage; none of the moldings match. The battered door that opens onto the grass courtyard has a glass top panel, and its screen door sets at a different slant than the inner door. In fact all the doors and doorways are slightly on the bias, in old adobes a common trait. Old, mismatched and much worn sofas and wooden chairs. Scattered rugs and blankets, always in lumps.

The roof leaks.

The outside doors are painted green, and a chile ristra swings in the wind. Evening dims.

Listening

I can't be quiet long enough.
A hundred generations.

Since we stopped being hunters,
who among us can keep still?

There is so much sound
in silence.

I love the bowl
for what it does not hold.

Totting up my business expenses, I found a receipt from the University Bookstore that read, "Prince of Darkness, $0.52."
    Seems underpriced.

From a neighbor, with coffee and a sit-down:
    In the 1770s the people of what is now Placitas lived in a walled Hispanic town called San José de Las Huertas. It was north of the basalt dyke with the petroglyphs—Cerro Negro—and north of the creek, "across from the tipis and a half mile west of the hippie encampment." Wherever *that* is.
    In 1823, Apache raids forced the Las Huertas settlers to move down to the Rio Grande at Algodones, where they lived for about twenty years. In the late 1830s it was safer to live unfortified, and they moved back and founded five villages: Ojo de la Casa, Tejón, Tecolote, San Pedro Rancho, and San Antonio de Padua de las Placitas.
    Again: until the Civil War, Placitas had no church—hence the supposed infant burial under my floor—so a traveling priest would come now and then to give services in a small chapel or private home. That was when a Placiteño who died had to be tied to a ladder and carried sixteen miles down the arroyo to the church at San Felipe Pueblo.

But where were people buried between the 1860s and the 1920s, the earliest dates I could find in the Catholic camposanto? Sixty years unaccounted for: that's a lot of dead folks. Maybe their gravesites were marked with wooden crosses, long erased by weather and time.

Santo Domingo Pueblo was the local headquarters for the Spanish Inquisition. Indians were hanged there. No wonder Santo Domingo became conservative, unwelcoming to anthropologists and linguists.

At the extreme southwest end of Cerro Negro are petroglyphs: crude masks, snakelike things, quadrupeds, a mountain lion, geometrics, and birds. There are also Christian crosses, pecked by Hispanic settlers to drive away the pagan devils associated with the old images.

In a gap on the Cerro Negro is a round stone structure whose door faces south. A shepherd's shelter? A hunting blind? Near it are many pecked crosses. Farther north and up on a high ridge is another structure, bigger and square, whose door faces more or less east.

Pecked on a rock, four bird feet and a small right hand.

Ancestors I

This purity,
though dead
or because dead:
the mark
of a red mud hand
no longer
yours
but the stone's.

Ancestors II

We love you.
Because we never knew you,
this is easy.
Heat, stink, terror,
sick panic of regret:
all wind.
Your bones are so clean.

Last night as I sat reading in bed a great horned owl called: *Hu-hu, hu-hu.*

I thought about the Navajo and European beliefs that the owl is a portent of death or witchcraft; about the owl as the Mother's bird; about the wise owl. I opened the door and spoke into the dark: "You are just what you are."

Boquillo the Cat
carried off by a great horned owl

You'd learned to hike
like a spaniel, talk
like a used-car salesman.
You were fourteen
and running out of challenges.
No wonder you went out
on that full moon night
and learned to fly.

In the middle of the night I woke to the church bell ringing. Next morning I went to look: the bell rope was loose and the bell stood upside down.

Cerro de Mañana is changing color toward spring, the junipers deep green, the haze of grass a frosty sage.

WHAT THE SYCAMORES FRAME AT SIX O'CLOCK . BETSY

Morning. The air smells wet, clouds hang heavy and gray. To the west there's sun on Cabezón and the plains are pink and white and yellow, Easter colors.

A neighbor from New England said, "The robins are back!"

They've been here all winter. Did he just now notice because spring is when you're supposed to see robins?

Jerusalem crickets squashed on the village street, rabbits squashed on the highway. Spring roadkills.

This morning, the first strolling pillbug. This afternoon, roses leafing out. First dandelion. First springing grass.

There is one junco still at the feeder.

Brilliant, late-afternoon light.

Along the main road the arroyo is many-branched, crumbly-sided and so deep, fifteen or twenty feet, that the cottonwoods along its bottom are all but hidden. Long sedge grows along the small, quick stream; fallen leaves are thick. Down there an orange cat walked alone. I whistled and it froze, stared, ran. It's a cat world with a maze of paths beside the stream, a secret labyrinth that penetrates the village.

Surely people once fetched their water from the stream, though now they all have wells or are on the iodine-flavored village water supply. The arroyo has gone back to its animal users and its generations of pottery, bottles, junked cars. It collects history and time and secrets the way it collects water.

To a bland glance from a passing car the arroyo seems to appear and disappear, surface and sink, bite and pierce into new territories. It is slowly eroding the village. In time, it will swallow it.

Finch

The sun is bright.
The door is open.
How many springs?
All that living craziness
comes again down the pike
as if there were a goal.
This is the goal:
the new pink finch
at the feeder,
who does not
remember
fall.

I thought I saw a hummingbird. I put out the feeder, but so far it seems untouched.

The long, dreaming shoulder of the mountain, furred with low trees. Snow at its height.

A tremendous hail- and thunderstorm last night. The daffodils are bruised.

An article in the *Smithsonian* says the center of our galaxy lies in the center of the constellation Sagittarius. It's beyond the stars we can see, but we can look toward it.

April

Daylight shines through a hole in the portal roof of the little adobe across the street.

Roof

The roof leaks.
Spring pours its storms,
the plaster lies in a wet pile
turning back to sand.
When we stop shoring things up,
down they come,
relaxed into the shape
of these old hills.

Yesterday a friend and I hiked at the S-curves in pouring rain: shapeless and flapping in ponchos, slipping and staggering, red mud to our knees. At last we gave up, went to the Range Café in Bernalillo and ate onion soup with sage.

This morning as I walked the village street a group of four goats, all different colors, tiptoed about in the far pasture with plenty of room to be curious. Goats have a quickness, like deer. A family of fat quail bustled among the Gambel oak and fallen leaves. These were bigger than the quail of my more northern childhood and had bleach-blond topknots. If I were a coyote I'd love to catch one.

Ah. They are scaled quail.

There are still a few juncos.

Last year's apples smell like cider vinegar.

I walked around the base of Cerro de Mañana. Above the arroyo there's a stone structure built into the living rock. Too new to be pre-Columbian. A sheep pen?

On the arroyo-bitten llano many chert flakes carpet the poor, gnawed soil. Are there buried pit houses? I know from archaeological field survey that a pit house can leave hardly a trace beyond flakes and a few potsherds. Its history is hidden.

I spoke at length, in Spanish, with the local go-to fixit guy: Manuel from Mexico, a witty, sagacious man in his fifties. I told him where in Mexico I had worked. He had never heard of it. He laughed and said, "What do I know? I've never been anywhere but Durango and Placitas."

He described himself as "muy católico." He didn't like to work on Sundays, he said, but often that's when people need him. I said, "Why don't you slip over to the chapel when the church bell rings?" He laughed again. "They'd think, 'That dirty Mexican, he doesn't even wash his face.'" His face was clean.

It's bad in Durango, he said. Drought, no work, people getting terrible diseases. He knows two who have horrible deformities, their tongues too big for their mouths. "Even grown people are getting smallpox, la viruela." In Mexico smallpox was eradicated in 1951. Poor vaccination rates among the rural poor, so maybe it's chicken pox, devastating in an adult?

I gave him my Spanish copy of *Donde No Hay Doctor,* and thought about the slow mixing of blood in Placitas. Settlers trudging up from Mexico, calling themselves Spanish but already mixed with Moors and Jews fleeing the Inquisition, Nahuatls and Tarascans and Huichols from Mexico, then intermarrying with Sandia Pueblo and later with French Huguenots and Lebanese and the Italians who came to raise wine grapes. The East thinks of itself as a melting pot, but New Mexico has a different recipe.

In 1620 when the Pilgrims stepped off Plymouth Rock—if they had kept walking west they could have come to Sunday dinner in New Mexico.

On the upper road before sunrise, among the oak brush, the skunky damp smell of spring.

Yesterday was the cooperative village ditch cleaning. The dead leaves pulled out of the acequias were dumped in the potholes of the dirt roads. The water in the ditch beside the red road, which had flowed all winter, was shut off so the cleaning gang could deepen the shallow place at the curve.

Max says, "Weather the last week of Lent is always nasty. After that it seems like it's a brand new season."

Spring Rain, Placitas

These sounds
will outlast us:
water striking earth,
feet of moths
at the window screen,
feet of birds:
cold, quick, small
on the wet ground.

Remember the color of daffodils at dusk.

In the field below the land grant spring there's a stone circle. The apparent doorway, a sort of vestibule, faces east. Perhaps the foundation of a brush shelter?

The stones are not fallen or scattered, just a ring. Until Prohibition that field was a vineyard of the old Mission grapes—a few scrawny vines still hang on—so whatever that ring was it's probably not old, or even associated with the vineyard. Maybe a tipi ring from the hippie era? Lying next to it were eight sun-eaten condoms, still in their wrappers.

Walkabout on a Saturday morning. I cut across several shallow arroyos with their rusty tin can dumps. In one was a squat, pressed glass bottle about two and a half inches high, a cream server from a fifties restaurant:

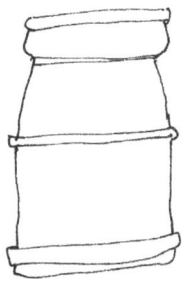

And three mother-of-pearl buttons, their shirt long gone.

As I hiked the ridge above the road to Tecolote I almost fell into another open mineshaft. *Damn.* I couldn't see the bottom. I dropped rocks and guessed maybe thirty feet down to some obstruction where the rocks bounced once, then twice more. Nobody would ever find you.

Up-down-up-down, over rills and arroyos to a ridge that paralleled the road almost to Las Huertas Creek. As I came down off the end of it I found, broken in two and ground into a dirt driveway, a worked obsidian flake:

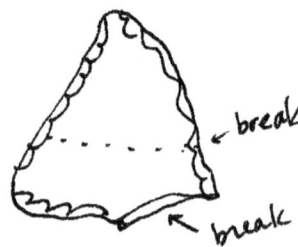

Where Las Huertas Creek road bears left it dawned on me that I was looking at the cholla-clotted ruins of what seemed to be a Puebloan structure rebuilt as a Hispanic house. A half dozen rooms built of river cobbles, a big ashy midden full of Puebloan potsherds, iridescent old glass, and white-and-blue glazed pottery bits that sure looked old to me. I don't know that I could recognize Majolica, that earliest pottery from Spain.

What once stood there?

Beyond it was a dump from the seventies that will be a boon to archaeologists in another half century. I found out what twenty years of desert sun does to a teddy bear.

I trudged up the hideous new scar of the road up the hill from Tecolote. There was a big gate across it, and lots of recent trash. Then back along the dusty road home, the wind in my face.

Soft moon, hushy wind. Lilacs.
  The cottonwood leaves are little.
  First crickets.

On Reading Earth History

Everything I am—
this hand, this thigh—
was blasted particles
spinning in enormous space.

I listen to wind blow
across a blue mesa,
both hands
still.

May

Rain rattles on the silver-gray plastic window sheeting. Wind, hush and hush. Where my corn patch was the new little green poplar bends and bows. It's a green, wet world, winter in the throes of turning summer, a cold spring. Wet hummingbirds make passes at the window glass: through it they can see the one red geranium bloom.

A sudden gust, hiss and bluster. *Tink, tank* of drops on the tin heater pipe. Indoors: quiet.

Before I left for the last Night Dance at Zuni I took a walk along the crooked red road. In the field below the malachite digging I noticed, on the hill east of the old concrete foundation, what are probably mine workings. On the north side of another hill are two big drystone walls. Why hadn't I seen them, in a hundred, two hundred walks? Had I never used my eyes?

I think of Dad's proverb: El que sabe, ve; él que no sabe, no ve nada. One who knows, sees; one who doesn't know, sees nothing.

What *do* I see?

At dusk the summer's first nighthawk fell about in the sky, crying its *Beent! Beent!* Now, in the later dark, a common poorwill shouts.

Nighthawk

Living in the world
by being small
and keeping still.
Like a nighthawk's egg—
fragile, speckled,
laid on the bare ground.

The many-coloredness of trees: all green but different shades, silver, gray, yellow, olive, blue.

So many small lives are strolling about: sowbugs, stinkbugs, ants. The poorwill is a nighttime regular.

In the apple tree there's a western tanager: bright green-yellow breast, bright red head. Downright tropical.

A scrub jay landed plonk on the window feeder and pecked up oatmeal with its long black bill. It looked at me with its liquid eye, then jumped away in a burst of wings. Some bird is yelling in bouts, as though it were being firmly squeezed.

I hiked up Cerro Escalera, east of Las Huertas Creek. Below, in what was the settlement of Ojo de la Casa, I could see the trace of what looked like a little racecourse: a pale oval that filled a whole field. Is that what it was? In the eras before television these communities entertained themselves. Surely they raced horses?

Down the arroyo someone is burning a heap of trash. The flames are bright daylight orange against greasy black smoke that rises straight up.

Saw: a barn swallow.

Heard: a black-headed grosbeak.

Last night at three in the morning I woke to a strange, half-rhythmic knock outside my window. Not animal. I couldn't imagine what it was. I got over my midnight cowardice and stuck my head out the window to hear water rushing in a pipe.

With flashlight and flipflops I went to see. A gasket on the irrigation pipe had burst and a four-foot rooster tail of water banged the rocks and sprayed into the street. There was nothing I could do in the dark, so I slapped a flagstone over the spray and went back to sleep.

Come morning, even after the pipe was fixed, it seemed the whole world was full of water: spitting by the reservoir, dripping in the salamander grotto, knocking and booming in the flume that runs along the crooked red road.

In all this wetness a rabbit hopped off, not far, and sat looking at me. Its back was the color of the damp earth, but its white scut gave it away. What is the evolutionary purpose of scuts, I wonder? To give the coyote a fair shake?

Rabbit

You are so little.
Everybody eats you.
Your ordinary day—
breakfast, sleep and joy—
is spent under winged shadows.
Hawk stoops.
Owl floats down.
Death for you is perfectly
certain, certainly
soon.

Do you worry?

Brisk, shy, small,
you eat flowers and sometimes
bounce as light and high
as a rubber ball.
I watched you creep
under a low leaf:
you laid your ears back flat.
You are careful.
When you can,
you run away.
When I meet you I always say,
"Don't run, bunny.
It's okay."
Still as a stone,
you stare back
out of your bright round eye.
Do you know I speak the truth?
Do you know I lie?

Early summer, a New Mexico afternoon. I walked the mail to the post office, the air full of drowsiness between heat and shadow. Grass moved in the moving air.

Smell of water: two thin men watered the chapel's hedge of pink roses and worked the ditch with shovels and unfriendly looks. Thunderheads bulked in the west. A timelessness, bleached wood bleaching paler in the sun. Siesta, the hour of sleep after the midday meal—as though that hour were here ingrained in the earth.

This morning I carried down off Cerro de Mañana an armload of stakes and sun-rotted white plastic. An aerial survey marker.

A chilly river of air from the open door pools around my bare ankles. I stop writing, put on socks.

The morning candle flame is pink.

It's all right sometimes to pull up the literal or intellectual as a tool, but let it submerge again immediately. That's the writer's mantra: "Show, don't tell."

Another way to say this is that living is best done in the flesh.

Rushing water in arroyo and acequia. On Paseo de San Antonio someone has built a toy water wheel in the ditch in front of their house. Hesitantly, it turns.

At the Catholic graveyard by the post office a shirtless man was hoeing weeds: Arsenio, who tends the roses at the church. I didn't recognize him at first and apologized, saying, "I only know who you are if you whistle."

He nodded at the graveyard. "Can't whistle here." In Anglo folklore you whistle as you pass a graveyard to keep the ghosts away. In Placitas, as in Zuni, does whistling *attract* ghosts? Or did he mean it was disrespectful?

In the Gilbert Islands of the Pacific, it's the ghosts themselves who whistle. Same in the Solomon Islands. Are there ghost dialects, in which some hate whistling and flee it, but some love it and come? In the Gilberts, said Sir Arthur Grimble, there's a ghost that smells terrible. Cada cual tiene su gracia.

Arsenio said the young men are lazy, they won't help him clean the graveyard even when he offers to pay them.

As I went along home, a quick-eyed swallow perched on the phone wire.

From a neighbor, more history:

The mine—the one with the big headframe?—across from Ojo de la Casa is the Montezuma mine. "It was begun in the 1890s. Lew Wallace came to visit it while he was writing *Ben Hur*"—well, no, since he left in 1881 and never came back. He hated New Mexico.

The family that's mostly in Tecolote now is Taraddei. I remember it from the gravestones in the camposanto. Italian winemakers, then big distillers during Prohibition. The "water holes" upcanyon, which a man warned a hiker friend and me away from, were mine tunnels that struck water that's now used for irrigation. The square holding tank was built for them.

Every human being has three or four years of almost total amnesia. For those missing years they have only subliminal and somatic memory.

Those years are the most important learning years in this creature's life. The time in which one's entire perception of being and universe is framed is precisely the time which one does not consciously remember.

Esto encierra un misterio.

2 kinds of grass + neighboring rock

June

The Indian rice grass begins to drop its fuzzy seeds. They taste like wheat. Its stiff little awns stick in the tongue; it needs to be parched with hot stones and ground to flour, the way the Archaics did.

How beautiful the mixing of human DNA. In a shop in Bernalillo, a man pure New Mexico: slim and tall, long black ponytail, slight beard and mustache, a round young face with a cleft chin and huge, Byzantine eyes. Helpful, well-spoken.

Just after sunset a big wind rushed up the valley, tossing the trees. It had come all the way from Cabezón, and will make falling asleep so pleasant. The white paper blinds are lowered, each with a square of sky above it, and the flame of the white candle in the green glass dish, wavering, casts a watery clear light.

I'm pretty sure the bird I saw balancing and yodeling on a phone wire was a northern mockingbird.

That wild-white-hair-pussytail grass, needle-and-thread grass. By curling and uncurling its tail with the moisture of the slight dew, the seed drills itself into the dirt.

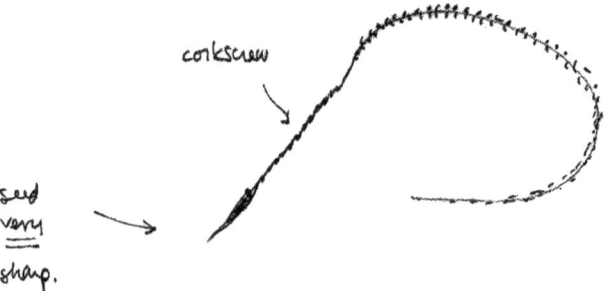

corkscrew

seed
very
sharp.

How to recognize the ruin of a prehistoric fieldhouse: wolfberry, cholla, and saltbush growing out of a little pile of rocks. Neighbor Bill Dunmire—he co-authored *Wild Plants of the Pueblo Province*—says those three "indicator plants" together are 100% indication of a ruin. More reliable even than potsherds.

A curved-bill thrasher nests in our cholla.

This morning, killed on the road: a strange, colorless, wormlike snake, its head almost indistinguishable from its tail except for its poor pale, forked tongue, which hung out. It was perhaps six inches long. Ants were eating it. My best guess is that it's a New Mexico blind snake.

Tomorrow is Día de Fiestas, the feast of St. Anthony. The village is a globe of sound, all birds and hammers.

A nine-year-old neighbor child informs me that she and her friend are playing detectives, that I am a supermodel and I have just been murdered.

I'm flattered. I wish I'd worn a classier bra.

Buffalo gourd with its orange, bell-shaped, stinking flowers crawls up the chain link fence. Its leaves are a powdery, bluish green. Next to it a cracked auto taillight glows in the morning sun like a broken ruby.

The junipers are flocked with tetones, cottonwood seed fluff, like light snow.

There are flickers in the cottonwood.

Flickers

People are clambering
in the summer trees.
If I could hold my heart
at a different angle, I could see
their houses, ladders,
roads and fields—
a vertical country
only partly ruled
by gravity.

Hot morning. Stripes of sun. The adobes are so full of the day's heat that at night they bake the sleeper like a bun.

Geese step in the shadows.

July

In the fine dust of the Oso Spring road, the handsome palm prints of a raccoon.

Two goats, tethered at a gate, say, "*Mmaa-oh.*"

Last night, the first good rain. There's mud in the street. The air is thick; walking feels like wading. All greens are darker. Blue-gray, which has no place in early summer, is dominant.

Men are restuccoing the Catholic mission. One of them, shirtless, bore the scar of a triple bypass. He said the church hadn't been thoroughly stuccoed since the 1940s. Where the skin of plaster was pulled off you could see the building's skeleton: windows that were lower than they are now.

Sidehilling along the highway, I spotted the scattered stones of a three-to-six-room ruin. A fieldhouse? Forty or fifty yards west of it was an Archaic site: patches of burned dirt, many flakes, no potsherds. (Most of the Archaic was pre-pottery.) Round and square manos, all broken. I had a very good time.

The evening has a sadness, as evening always has. I'd stopped at the graveyard on the way home. One child's grave had a homemade headstone with a cross fashioned of tiny clear marbles—fashionable in the sixties for the cracked-marble jewelry I'd made with neighbor girls—inset in concrete. The grave of the little girl supposedly beaten to death by her family was swamped with teddy bears, porcelain angels, baskets of artificial flowers. Guilt, awe, pity, fear? I felt all four.

Morning walk in Placitas Heights. It's too new. But the mountain is beautiful and close, and the sky is big.

A fat jackrabbit with a big round eye leapt up and ran *toward* me, staring as it passed.

Our two pairs of jungle fowl, with minds of their own, have escaped into the arroyo to do their goofy cluck-and-cock-a-doodle for the whole neighborhood, like it or not. They are pretty chickens, brisk and slim, without the down-at-heel, slatternly look of some hens.

It rained hard in the night. In the morning a brilliant bit of rainbow stuck out of the mountain crest like a feather.

The trunk of the New Mexico locust in the lower garden has starry clusters of thorns. Some are five inches long. Why did I not notice them before?

Grasshoppers have stripped the leaves from one of the apple trees.

The sun goes down in windy, jumbled clouds. Bit by bit the night comes.

The old vines along the fence of the crooked red road have grapes on them. Not ripe yet. For the first time I looked beyond them and saw that the whole field used to be a vineyard. Here and there, there are still stubby, stunted vines.

Are those next to the road bigger because the road diverts water?

The old cottonwood at the crook in the road had a Budweiser can jammed into a knothole. While I pried it out I looked into the arroyo. There were plenty more cans, as well as the scattered, rain-sodden gear of the two little girls who play house down there.

Dark Placitas. The other night I heard a man scream—in our arroyo, I thought. The house was full of visitors and other sleepers; I stepped among them quietly, locking doors. Sometimes at night boys pull the rope of the church bell. It rings out with solemn, erratic strokes. They leave the bell standing upside down.

Evening. The sky going opal in the west, fading to the purplish blue that is seen, I think, only in the desert. I'm looking out over the Jemez, listening to our new chickens—Bertha, Irma, and Firma, named by a six-year-old—peep quietly to each other in adolescent Chickeneze.

BERTHA's ———>

The
strawberry
blonde

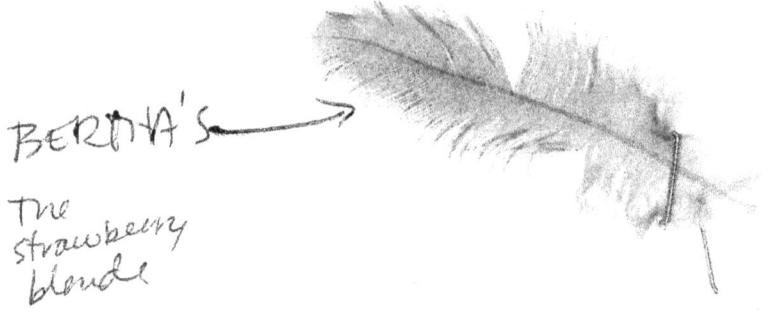

Roadkill at the bottom of Dome Valley road: a four-inch centipede thing, with stripes. There was still some reaction left in the tail end. As the ants got to work it shivered and waved its legs.

A neighbor says there was a man—maybe in his dad's time?—who had separated early from his wife. She was a pretty, guera, rosy-cheeked woman, "a real Spaniard," and every morning the husband would go over to her house for coffee. Sooner or later they'd get into an argument and she'd yell, "Get your ass out of here!" He'd run, she'd grab the pistol and fire after him—"and she was a good shot!"—until he'd escaped to his house. Next morning it would happen all over again.

Small town life.

Star Wars on the patio. The hummingbird feeder, usually the scene of placid arguments between six or eight black-chinneds, has been commandeered by a furious male rufous. His hum is loud and he curses constantly, a red bullet zipping through the crowd. At rest he sits *on* the feeder.

I watched him put out his tongue, thin as a hair.

> A feather fell
> from a hummingbird's wing.
> I looked and looked
> but never found it.

Summer wind hums in the phone wires. Grass and willow bend, show silver. Faintest spice of dew. Starlings are clamped stolidly to the phone wires.

A soft, haughty, secretive cat.

Another mantis on the hummingbird feeder. Buff, small, with a turned-up tail. I deported it. Now I wish I'd left it alone and watched.

August

A deluge. "Male rain," we say in the Southwest. The arroyo runs with brown water.

A twenty-eight-inch rattler is dead in the road above the arroyo, its head crushed. Fawny desert colors, and a tail not black like a blacktail, not Koshare-striped like a western diamondback. A prairie, I guess.
   Yellowjackets, bright yellow and black, feed on its body.

In the garden dirt of the churchyard there are cellophane-like sheets of mica, an inch and a half square. I thought they might be from an old window, but house windows in early New Mexico weren't made of mica, as non-geologists will tell you, but of selenite. The mica is probably from a window in the door of a long-discarded cast iron stove.

August 10 is Día de San Lorenzo, Bernalillo's festival day and the anniversary of the Pueblo Revolt. The Matachines will be danced both days at the "wache," the Bernalillo spelling of a Pueblo word that means "storehouse" and refers to the southernmost neighborhood of Bernalillo, the old town.

In Bernalillo, Matachines celebrates the escape of the local families during the Pueblo Revolt: they were so intermarried with Sandia Pueblo that the rebel Indians just let them pass. The Monarca is Montezuma; the little girl is Marina or La Malinche; the Bull is Evil; the Abuelo is the taskmaster with a whip, much like the Hopi whipper kachinas.

The gossip is that last year they reinstituted an old custom, the *actual* castration of the bull at the end of the dance. Yikes. Is that so?

A big meteor. It left a whitish streak behind it like a contrail. The mosquitos were biting so I came back in.

There

I let my whole face look up
into the round night and saw
 a star rush across the dark.

A ladder-backed woodpecker, walloping away at a phone pole.

I took my walk in a fine, persistent female rain. A neighbor complimented me on braving the weather. "Rain's good, though," she said. "My lawn, I can find it."

A lean gray blur in the headlights, a coyote ran across the road in search of a housecat snack.

Woke to thunder.

From the Tunnel Springs trailhead I hiked off-trail and found a couple of creepy, black-mouthed mine adits. No thanks. Trotted back to the car and went instead to Las Huertas, where I stumbled on a tiny Puebloan field house built of red stone, still a nice square shape. Next to it lay a comal of yellow-green sandstone, also chipped square.

Made it home *just* as it started to pour.

Saw a lesser goldfinch.
   Lesser than what?

Rained all night. Mist on the mountain's shoulder. The trunks of the cottonwoods in the arroyo are black with rain.

Composting

On a day when the day
though rich is so much
the compost heap while the heat
the maggots the hens the minute
unmakers set their mouths
to disassemble everything I named,
I must sit among death
dead: arms, legs and tongue
departing to be used
by small beings who do not
know me and do not care.
If there were ever doubt
that we belong not to
ourselves or to some cleanly god
with calipers and a book
but only, only
to this place, this huge,
inter-opportunistic dance
that eats and shits,
if there were ever doubt
that we are each other,
here
that doubt dies, too.

I removed yet another mantis from the hummingbird feeder. This one was medium-sized and green.

When frightened, the geese run like fat ladies who aren't used to running. Their fat bounces around.

September

A tarantula crossed the road. Must be September.

A neighbor told me that in the sixties there was a nudist colony in a huge old tree just west of the Tunnel Springs road.

In a *tree*? Ow.

The locally grown dope was called Placitas Train Wreck. Most of it was grown by guys whose wives were nurses who worked in town. The men worked a little construction. The neighbor said pot is still grown here, indoors or underground.

A windy, cloudy day, after the beautiful one I spent working indoors.

I headed for Tunnel Springs. Stopped at the B&B, Hacienda de Placitas. The owner is a bonny Frenchman with a gold chain. He says there is the ruin of an old house on the property and, up and down the arroyo, five coal mines. He had no objection to people hiking on the other side of the arroyo—heck, it wasn't his land!

I hiked the steep route above Tunnel Springs trail, so-called Rheumatoid Gulch. The piñones had just come ripe, there'd been a wind, they were all over the ground, and the jays were going crazy. I beat them to a pound and a half.

In a nondescript spot about ten feet off the trail I found one silver Hopi earring. I bet its owner had left the trail to pee; that's how I found it.

On the Crest a little kestrel sailed sideways in the wind.

It's raining beautifully in the dark. I've put on wool socks.

A great commotion among the sparrows. From the phone line a pretty kestrel, perhaps a relative of the one on the Crest, is staring into the patio and fluffing its cream-colored pantaloons.

A neighbor says the reservoir on the Dome Valley road is called Tanque del Oso, Bear Pond, and the more southwesterly one above the kink in the road is Tanque de la Ciruela, Cherry Pond. There must be wild cherries there.

The little acequias that come off the main ditch are "sangrias." The overflow is "desague." He told me the word for the ditch gate you lift to let the water in, but I've forgotten it. "Atarque"?

Chilly. Sunflowers and purple asters. This final blast of flower-energy—how do the plants have time to get seeds made before the frost? Everything weedy, wild, and harsh is flowering. So much of it is yellow: chamisa and snakeweed and yellow daisies.

Then it's dying season. Time to die like the sunflowers, to make room for new growth.

I wandered off the Dome Valley road and into the big field below the spring. A raven sat down on a tree and began to talk: gargle, gurgle, giggle, rattle, clonk. It teetered and yakked and stuck out its neck feathers and clapped its bill until I could see the red color inside it. It was funny in itself, and doubly funny because tonight I'm having dinner with a friend whose nickname is Raven.

Later, on a whim, I parked at the base of the S-curves, walked two ridges east, and returned to the car with my—sandaled—toes full of cactus spines.

A Maynard Dixon sky, blue and pink and purple behind spitting rain. Distant lightning, cloud trailing through a fire sunset, wind blowing this way and that. The mountains are velvet shades, with autumn colors starting at the Crest. The Del Agua aspen are beginning to turn.

A wonderful day, spent all by myself. From home I walked to just above the B&B and crawled arroyo and hillside, around and about, for a couple of hours. The coal mines were clearly visible. A jackrabbit zipped away.

Back in the village I cut through a friend's backyard, up and over the ridge behind the village street, then west over the next ridge. Potsherds all over the place, but no sign of any structure. Where did the potters shelter from the rain?

Came home sunburned, happy.

A big fat red-shafted northern flicker, flying phone pole to phone pole, yelling.

October

The gray cat who showed up two weeks ago, demanding food—I have been feeding her obediently—turns out to belong to Matt-down-the-street, one of the owners of the Range Café. Her name is AWOL.

Time is passing and passing. I feel it flow past my shoulders like the current of a river.

The cottonwood in the upper field is bright yellow against a black trunk.

A half-dead centipede in the dirt road, the translucent yellow of a cheap plastic pipestem.

I can see my breath.

Night. Snow on the ground, thin and shifting; a cold, urging wind. The room is drafty; the heater roars. I bought a roasted chicken at the market. I feel safe and warm and fed in the heart of the storm.

Our stubborn unroasted chickens refuse the coop and roost in the apple tree. Will their feet freeze?

November

I'm in New York City. What can I say?

December

A mouse is a tiny, unimportant thing, yet it is just as much "a lot" as a city full of people.

Yesterday, hiking, I *stopped* and drew.

Each drawing was of a tiny neighborhood, a community of beings. A distinct, intimate, real place.

There was a little hill with seven clumps of grass on it. Now I wish I'd drawn it.

what a portion looks like by itself.

So mild and still, it seems like some motionless non-season. It makes me uneasy. We need darkness, cold, snow, closure, sleep. Not this suspension that feels like stasis, hypnosis. The robins' sound is springlike, but pale as winter sunlight.

Send us water from the sky.

In the road below Tanque del Oso I found what looks like a piece of turquoise, but unworked—a little pebble.

Bertha the Sex-Change Chicken, overcome with her new testosterone, hopped the fence and disappeared—into a coyote, I assume. Damn good thing. She'd been crowing at forty-five minute intervals all night long.

This morning, near the top of the village road, I heard the telltale bark-squeak of a coyote on Cerro de Mañana. Far away there, a big tan dog was chasing or following a coyote, also big, gray with a black tip to its brush. They'd run a little, then the coyote would stop, half turn around, and look back.

At about the same time I heard another coyote, very near, perhaps just over the ridge from the high field. Bark, bark, squeak. Were they talking? Luring the dog, which seemed unhurried and surely was big enough to defend itself?

Big gray coyote, running along the side of a hill.

New to New Mexico

What I shall never have:
a house built of mud
made from the dust
of my mothers' bones.

I shall be the first
to be eaten by Coyote.

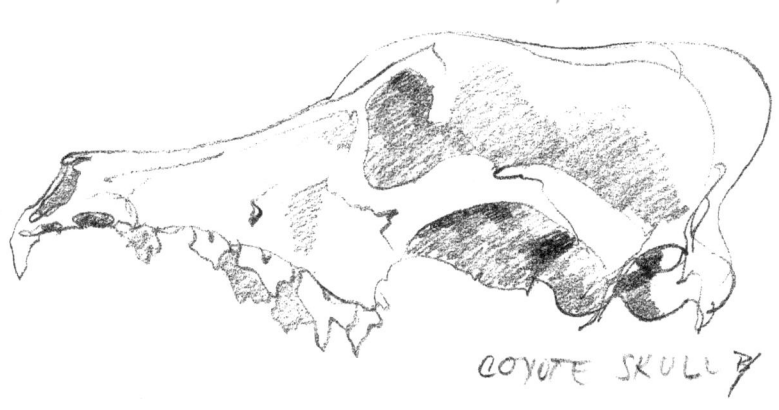

COYOTE SKULL

A hike to Tapia Wash, out by Cabezón, fell through. Grumpy, I set off alone up Tunnel Springs trail. At the easternmost bend I took off cross-country toward Tanque de la Cereza. There I saw:

Another hill with seven humped clumps of grass.

A thick, thick clump of cholla living and dead.

The varied, flat, circling mesas at the foot of the Jemez Mountains.

Trees as individuals.

The proportion of trees to ground: how they live with each other as a community, at a social distance.

Terra-cotta pink grass.

A spiral snail shell, cross-sectioned, perfect, in a big gray limestone boulder:

I came home comforted, in a better mood.

My heart is not a stone.
It feels alive.
But such a dense,
slow life:
a bristlecone pine's.

Oh wonderful! On the uphill leg of the La Cereza road, in a Russian olive, were thirty to fifty mixed robins and cedar waxwings, so busy eating they paid no attention to me at all. Hops and flutters and low chat. Rejected seeds pattered down in a steady rain.

January

Another mild, pale, still morning. The horehound and thyme on the patio were so dry I watered them with a bucket. There's an old hiking boot over the garden spigot to keep it from freezing.

This bland, pale weather goes on and on.

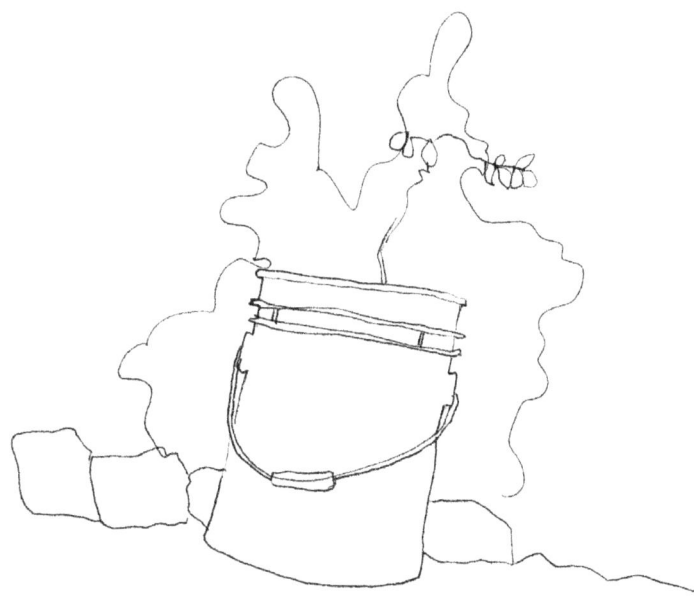

Short, sweet, alone, up Tunnel Springs trail.

A mild day of soft breezes, too warm in two sweaters. I drew my seven clumps of grass. The hill they are growing on turned out to be the spoil heap of a prospect hole.

I left the trail to wander the arroyos. Gathered eighteen flicker feathers, making up for a handful I lost three weeks ago. As I turned home I met on the trail a brisk, slender man in his thirties with a New Jersey accent, who carried his laughing black-haired daughter, perhaps eight years old, slung across his shoulders like a deer carcass. Her feet were tired, he said. Both seemed delighted by their cleverness.

The weather continues strangely nonexistent. Colorless. Dry.

There's been no weather for two months or more, a suspended calm so temperate that it seems neither hot nor cold. Today at five a wild wind tore through. It hurled up two months of dust and sand, grayed everything and brought an early dark. A spate of rain damped the dust. Now cold rises from the earth.

Year Three

February

I stopped to talk with the man who lives in the old house at the T of the village street—the house whose garden has shrines, iron frogs on loveseats, plaster donkeys, plastic ducks, sunflower pinwheels, weathered plastic saints. My kind of garden. He said his grandfather carried the mail Cabezón-Bernalillo-Placitas-Hagan, in little boxes, on a wagon and buckboard.

Windy, gray. The wall heater's pilot light keeps blowing out. This morning was shiny and blustery and bright, all soft like spring, and now a sad Februaryness has come wrestling back. The voices of the birds come muffled from beyond the wall.

A light dusting of snow. I hope against hope that something has eaten our loudmouth bronzy rooster, a.k.a. Macho Man. He didn't crow this morning, is nowhere to be seen.

I worry that I may not be paying attention as completely as I did when I first came to Placitas. A first year is a continual revelation; then you think you know what's going on, and stop seeing.

The truth is that I know nothing about this place. All I know is what is quickly and superficially available, culturally visible.

The many-layered, infinitely translucent reality of this earth and community are as fresh, as unseen as ever. They live in the angle of light, in sound and reverberation, in odor; in the texture underfoot, under hand or knee.

Populations live here about which I know nothing.

Ghost

Raise a new ghost
from an old foundation.

Someone died here.
These walls are their flesh.

The one-eyed god
still has a human shape.

Out of this sandy wall rise
not ancestors but spirits.

They lived here before us.
Now they watch.

I remember a hawk's feather
on a high cliff, teetering in wind.

There is nothing that does not come
out of silence.

This morning a little woodpeckerish pepper-and-salt creature was *brrr*-ing on the phone pole. Its bill was narrow as a nail. I said to it, "*Wackawacka!*" It scooted around back of the pole and flew off.

God be thanked! I'm sure something has eaten Macho Man. On Monday night he hullabalooed in the tamarisk as usual, but he hasn't been seen or heard since. I think of a great soft-winged owl.

At 1:30 a.m. I woke to a hen shrieking in the viny bush by the street fence. Thinking *weasel-skunk-badger*, I got up and looked out.

Full moonlight. Nothing. I looked up: a fat owl silhouette on the phone lines, a black bulk that, from its posture, looked down. After a few minutes it drifted off north. I went back to bed.

Half an hour later the hen yelled again, this time from under the tamarisk. The owl was perched on the sycamore, now turned to the moonlight. I fetched my borrowed binoculars and studied its ashy-moony face, watched it turn its head and look shadowy down. Its big ear tufts were like a cat's ears.

It flew off. I went back to bed and to sleep. Half an hour and alarms again, now from the viny bush. I couldn't see the owl; perhaps it was in the cottonwood. The hen broke across the open, clucking wildly, and made for the tamarisk.

Silence. Sleep. Come morning I expected to find her corpse, but she was scratching busily in the compost heap.

Hens

Most vulnerable of birds,
prey to owl and skunk and weasel,
coyote and the family dog.
We say hens are stupid.
Certainly they are not
intellectual. In their tiny wisdom
they peck and chat in the tall grass,
living perfectly their hens' life.

The goose is setting, and the gander has gone territorial. He hissed and honked at me; in the cold air after rain, out of his beak came clouds of goose breath.

March

A white guinea hen stood on our board fence and creaked. I have no idea who she belongs to.

How can a living being "belong to" anybody?

Too synchronous.

I went for a short climb on Cerro de Mañana. Halfway up I started to pick up what I thought were pheasant feathers: some long, floppy, and iridescent green, some short and bronzy.

Then I got it. Macho Man!

If they're not his, then an identical owl has eaten an identical rooster. They have the right amount of wear to have been out in the weather for two weeks.

But why were they exactly where I climbed the Cerro? I'd never gone that route before, probably never will again.

Grasses:

Terra-cotta-colored stuff : Little bluestem.

Sideoats grama :   (The one whose stem is left crooked
                      after the seeds fall, like:

Sleepy grass

Alkali dropseed :

                      ribbony leaves

Spring. The elm is full of green dots, not yet fallen, that will all
try to be trees. The air is soft, it stirs. Birds sing and sing. The
first daffodil looks like bunched fingers; the sheath is off but the
flower hasn't opened.

April

Daffodils last barely two weeks.
    Two weeks.

There's an inch of ice on the goose water.

Humans are no different from animals and rocks.

At any instant, the world is giving us something: a totality to be felt, moved with, received, recorded, acknowledged, made astonished by.
    We choose whether we will receive this, or whether we will bull on—trying to force what we "need to" do, "should" do, "must" do: make money, feel effective, accomplish what we expect of ourselves. And so on.
    Whereas the passion is in obedience: to offer oneself as the servant of what is given, the as-yet-unknown.
    Damn that sounds corny. A lot of true stuff does.

Huge, sloppy, goosefeather snow fell, then stopped. The world is gray and wet. The gander dunks his head in his water pot and scrubs his bosom with his beak. Firma-the-Hen croons, brisk little body. I'm still full of yesterday's hike, rich with it. From this wet back yard I see mesas where snow scuds among striped red rocks, foggy aspen still unleafed, the whiter-than-white flank of the mountain against an iron sky. Small figures plod there, self-contained.

I am so lucky.

When the goose gets up off her nest and comes to eat, the gander hollers. She has covered her four eggs with straw and her own soft down. Warm from her body: warm straw, warm down, warm eggs.

She is skinny and ratty and leaves the nest for barely ten minutes.

Firma Hen has big strong feet. She scratches vigorously, raises dust. She's quite conversational and croons when she is near me. I like her. She's a Barred Rock, I think.

Now I understand the Baba Yaga story, the witch's hen-legged house.

Sleepy, aching, sweet spring eases into early summer. Slight traffic passes on the road. The mountain shoulder is misted with dust. There's a suspended feeling, bird chant. In the front patio rosemary is blooming, dark green spikes and purple-blue flowers: vigorous after winter, a dry-and-hot-country plant. Also tulips, red and yellow and orange and bright white.

A lizard in the sun.

What's making distances so smoky? Are there fires in the Bosque?

I'm still in winter mode, which thinks there's no world outdoors except on weekends.

The gray cat, AWOL, has been ranging around the house. She lies stretched at my knee, then commandeers my lap.

At the bend of the red road near the huge cottonwood, a favorite place for teens to drive their ancient cars, are five discarded condoms in four colors.

The roof of the adobe across the street is completely down, a heap of mud and sticks. The vigas are still whole. They bar the blue sky, which looks strange there, where there used to be a roof.

I am waiting for Firma to finish laying an egg for me to take to Zuni.

Last night the goose and gander were killed by dogs. Firma is nowhere to be found—killed or driven off.

There are goose feathers all over the hill, like an exploded featherbed. One lone goose egg lies in the middle of the yard.

> Little feet, I'm sad.
> You live such a short time
> and I so long,
> under this light
> that comes and goes.

May

A trip to the adobe yard.

Dirt for the bricks comes from Algodones. It's trucked in and dumped in heaps, then shoveled up and run through a pug mill, screened, mixed with water and straw and a bit of asphalt to increase its resistance to rain.

Hundreds of adobe molds, like ladders with seven rungs, are laid in rows. The process is primitive: a front-end loader shovels up the slop and dumps it onto the molds, where it's raked in with rubber-tipped hoes.

In a day or so the molds are pulled off. If it's rainy season or a rainy day, they'll just be loosened, then left to dry a little longer.

The bricks lie in long lines: Thursday's are wet, Wednesday's are damp, Tuesday's are dry. Monday's are dry enough to be stood on edge. Later they'll be stacked—some of them for as long as next winter, when, for their scarcity, they'll cost an extra ten cents each.

The yard workers are Mexican—young, dark, disdainful, strong. All wear straw hats. The owner is lean, wrinkled from the sun, a New Jerseyite in filthy jeans and a tie-dyed tee from the seventies. His house is full of happy, very green houseplants.

Hummingbird wars. Brisk and suspicious, the tiny sentinel is on his favorite perch, a bare twig at the top of the pear tree. The air is loud with buzz and squeak, as though he could use a drop of WD-40.

In the middle of the Dome Valley dirt road two paper roses had been planted upright, held in place by stones. Quite far apart—maybe two hundred yards? The yellow one had been run over but the pink one still stood straight, withered and shrunken by rain.

At eleven p.m. I finally tracked a twitching, scratching noise to a daddy longlegs catching a beetle on the paper window blind. Such a little thing to make such a racket!

June

Month of grasses. The stems are tall now and the seeds, all different kinds, are pushing out of their tight jackets. This morning I picked a stem that has sharp, long fuselage shapes emerging from its sheath in a fireworks pattern; tomorrow it will have a fringe of dangling seeds.

The foxtails are already yellow. In the desert you don't get to be tender for long.

In the red road lay a dead moth of that pale green color known to bath towel manufacturers as "sea foam." A little moth, with big, staring, dark green eyes.

Summer Afternoon

The old shirt slung
over the chair back
holds the shape
of my body, as though
in an instant I might rise
there, ghost or spirit,
and move about.
Sunlight walks across the floor.
In the distance
a neighbor whistles.

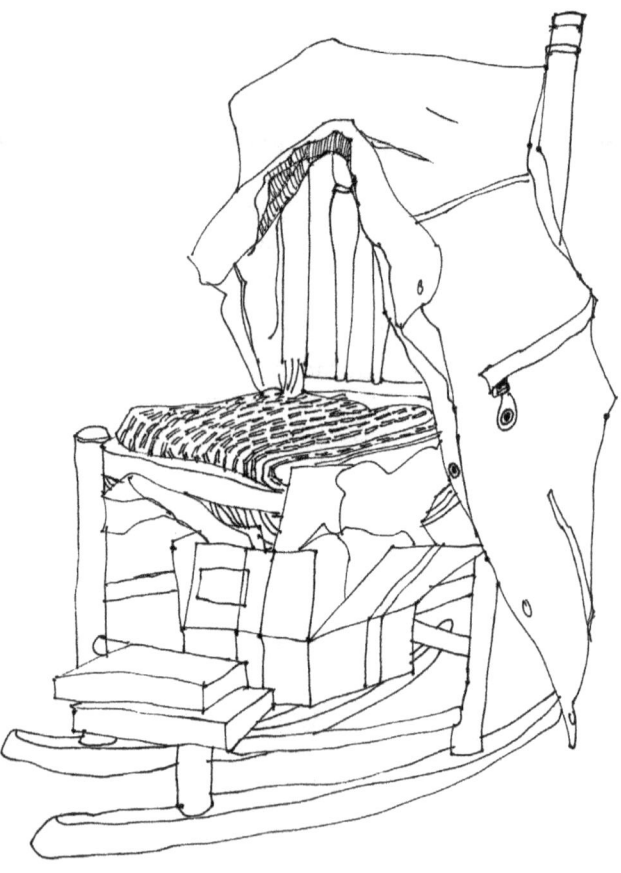

A stag beetle crossed the road, precise as a mechanical toy.

In our woodpile there is a feral mama cat, a Siamese, and her two marmalade kittens.

Once again the fuzzy-seeded Indian rice grass is coming ripe for Solstice. Also needle-and-thread grass with its spiral tail. The white-haired field shines in the morning.

A man from Dome Valley—he called it Doom Valley—stopped in his van while I was picking needle-and-thread grass. He asked whether I had found the grapevines: the field had been a vineyard, he said, but abandoned since Prohibition. The few vines still alive are Spanish Colonial grapes, once cultivated by the Christian Brothers. He had taken some cuttings, sprinkled them with root powder, and they grew. He said, "Anything that can survive in New Mexico for fifty years without water is *tough*."

Three windows wide open. A butterfly—dark, with yellow-edged wings—flew in and beat against the closed window and, softly, against my fingers when I caught it. It grew quiet. I let it go in the sun.

The band for the St. Anthony's Day fiesta, across the arroyo, is determined to play until everybody drops of exhaustion. It's been cranking nonstop since noon, and it's now past six, on the Sabbath no less. My Presbyterian ancestors are in a righteous hissy.

Tonight the waxing crescent moon looks pink. A long way west, Venus is bright.

The bindweed is flowering, many pinky-purple blossoms. Banks of it tie the woodpile to the ground, where the feral cat and her kittens live. It ties up the cholla hedge on the upper village road, prickly fierce cholla wrapped in green leaves and pink flowers.

Changing

The young hens have grown two sizes overnight.
Owls have not eaten them.
They scratch in the blue flax,
wind blows through the open window,
it is morning all over the world.
I am old. The cat is young.
In the woodpile's warren
she feeds on spring mice by hundreds.
The woodpile is bound to the ground
by morning glory.

In the shade of the lilac the hens are trying to perch together on the upturned washtub. They crowd each other off. They bang on the tub with their beaks as if it were a drum.

One of the places where we used to hike southwest of the city has been closed off, made into a landfill. Soon it will receive trainloads of used Pampers from New Jersey. In conjunction with it, three ranchers have padlocked the old road, even though fifty percent of that land is public.

Gates and bars and cages are clanging shut, fencing us away from the world.

In Dome Valley, another roadkill moth. Strange concept, that. I can't find the moth in my meager reference books:

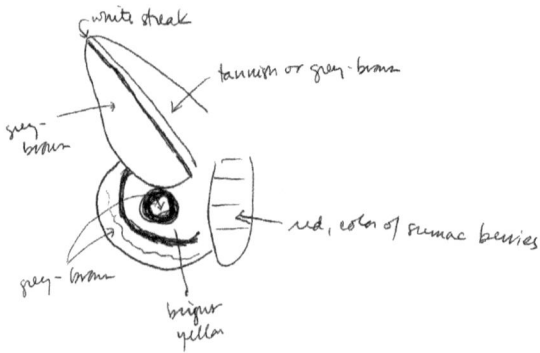

July

Placitas's tiny Fourth of July parade just straggled by: decorated bikes, a few lowriders, a few sweaty horses, a cavalcade of shiny Model Ts and the new fire engine with its siren blaring. Kids scurried around the road's edge, grabbing tossed lollipops and free ballpoint pens. I snagged a couple of caramels myself.

I was thinking, "If I were a man, today I'd go out into the silence of the desert." The truth is rather, "If it were safe for a woman to go alone into the desert, that's what I'd do today." Bitter truth: it's not safe for me to go there alone.

I'll go up Tunnel Springs trail instead.

Another beautiful moth, this one alive, sucking at the pomegranate blossoms. Pale pink-orange, with rusty highlights.

I started the day poorly and late. But a western tanager with its bright red head flew to the sycamore not ten feet in front of me. I had never seen one so close.

Afoot at last, I crossed the abandoned vineyard at the foot of Dome Valley road. A descanso by the highway that marks an old wreck was decorated with faded flowers of plastic and cloth, a cheap rosary with a plastic crucifix. The cross itself is white-painted chip-carved wood, the name now unreadable. I scrambled up jaggy rocks west of the highway, but found myself near someone's house and hastily slid back down.

Home again, footsore and pleased.

Monsoon clouds have begun to appear over the tip of the mountain. Yesterday afternoon about five they spread out, thundered, and let fall a solid male rain that turned female, gentle and full.

For weeks the world has been silent in the heat and drought, as though nothing were left but cicadas; this morning everything has found a voice, chirping and shouting. You can *feel* the earth drink and sigh. The air is odorous as skunk, a deep, complex, spicy smell.

The western tanager came back to my desk window for an instant. Later he teetered on a fence post, bright red head. On the Las Huertas Creek road I saw my very first Placitas roadrunner. So many fewer here than in the Valley. Perhaps it's the altitude?

As I walked past the abandoned vineyard a large bird—a jay?—soared in and carried off a nestling from the nest of a yellow warbler. The baby dangled from its claws. The mother bird shrieked and mobbed the robber, but it was implacable and flew off up the canyon. She came back, sailed around a little, sat on a phone wire, then took off again upcanyon in the direction of the predator.

It was quite impossible for me not to project my human feelings on that scene: the mother returning, sore-hearted and terrified, to the cold place in the nest. I imagine how, this morning when she woke with her fuzzy babies, she could not have suspected this would happen. I wonder and hope that she has other children ... and so on. I am not rejoicing any more in this day of first rain.

The Way It Was

As though I were the wire on which
messages pass through the cosmos:
traveling shudder
of the Big Bang,
shiver of leaf.
Morning thunder.
Rain
hushing the dry grass.

I watched a crowd of chickens that had gathered under a peach tree bowed with bright fruit. They made standing hops a foot straight into the air. Like popcorn—*boing! boing!*—nabbing a bite of peach with each hop.

Husk of a black stinkbug. Husk of a black stag beetle.

Took a walk with a friend up the village lane at the dark end of dusk. The nighthawks had already gone to ground. Suddenly, oddly, something flew across the road in front of us, chucking softly: a stocky bird that flew in low swoops as though it didn't want to leave the ground. It perched on the fence wire, then disappeared down the road to the orchard. It seemed late for it to be out. It was barely visible in the dark except for a white arc of feathers on the end of its tail.

I said, "Weird."

My friend laughed and said, playing Carlos Castaneda, "That's your ally."

A moment later it flew out of the orchard, still softly calling. It flew around our heads in a perfect circle, not five feet away. I spun, watching it. It flew back into the orchard.

What was it?

Magic!

I think it was a nightjar. Maybe. Or my ally.

Long Summer

The ninety days
of heat are ninety years,
each year a journey
from dark to light
to dark:
the chilly spring
of dawn on the laps of grasses,
the standing shaft of noon,
the dusk sewn down
in the west by the whine
of nighthawks' wings.

August

The church caretaker—Arsenio, the whistler—said that fifteen years ago or so somebody in the village kept a hundred goats ... at least I think that's what he said. The conversation was in early morning and Spanish, so it had vague spots. He told me the name of the cloud that pours over the mountain shoulder, signaling the end of the dry season and the beginning of the monsoon: la nube valdeza, the Valdez cloud. I wish I knew why. In my forays into the centuries-deep history of this place I am as random and small as a hen pecking up scratch.

Four of the latest chickens have gathered at my feet, hoping for a handout. Dobinde, the blackest one, is bravest. Her comb is pale pink. Kwili, pepper-and-salt, has a bright red comb.

Fire in the Sandias, in the ragged, rugged area of Piedra Lisa. A smudgy column of smoke drifts in the dry wind, with dirty, squirming billows at its foot. I parked and watched. Eerie, to see that change happening in the absolute silence of distance.

From a conversation:

- ⊚ On the old trail or road down Las Huertas Creek, are there descansos? If they carried the dead down to San Felipe on ladders, you'd think there would be.

- ⊚ Supposedly there are traces of old waffle gardens above the old San Juan de Las Huertas ruin, "down toward the creek from the L turn."

- ⊚ All along Las Huertas Creek below the ruins of Las Huertas there are Pueblo ruins.

- ⊚ There was a torreón to watch for Navajos attacks at the Angostura ford.

- ⊚ From the 1850s to the 1880s Santana Mill in Algodones served the Pueblos. It was enormous and mule-driven.

- ⊚ The old Angostura ford was formed by gravel washed down San Felipe arroyo.

Bang! A bird hit the bay window. It stood on the gravel, stunned, beak agape. I don't know what it was: striped black-and-white head, yellowy-brown underparts, a spotty-streaky breast. Beak hefty as a towhee's.

AWOL the cat was prowling, so I picked up the bird—it startled in my hands—and perched it out of cat reach in the tangle of a bridal veil bush. A few minutes later it was still there, eyes closed. I thought it was dead, but when I jiggled the bush it flinched and stared. Poor thing. In bird world either you're in roaring health or you're dead, there's not much wiggle room.

When I looked for it later it had flown. Good.

With not much time for a walk I planned to park near the junction of Las Huertas Creek and the school bus road, but on the way I passed Sasquatch, the tattered, filthy guy who walks the village in a dress. He's a holdover from Tawapa, what's left of the hippie commune established here in the sixties. Tawapa was its own story of delusions, murders, and folks who showed up at the post office stark naked, but I've encountered only shreds of gossip and a lingering local resentment. Sasquatch is harmless, but he was sitting by the road with another apparently drug-fried character whom I didn't recognize, so I drove past the commune area and parked where I thought, from descriptions, the site of San José de las Huertas might be.

I tried again to locate the square outline of the fortified village. No luck. Perhaps it's where the juniper and cholla are thickest, on the slight slope right next to the road?

Farther down the creek were long flat bluffs covered with ancient heaps of rock. The waffle gardens? Field houses? Field stone cleared for farming? The bluffs seemed too high and dry. There was a scatter of potsherds.

I drove as far as I could before I ran out of two-track. The creek bed stretched west, beautiful under its standing cliffs. On my way back, I paused again at the possible San José site, puzzled and frustrated. Above it on the creek was a small but *very* old ruin scattered with thick historic potsherds, red or white or black on red. A few chips of old green glass, iridescent with centuries. Had it lain looking at the sun since before the Pueblo Revolt of 1680?

En route home I stopped in Tecolote at the Taraddeis', the first time I'd been up that driveway with its old cribbed-log granary on four wooden legs. There was fruit for sale: peaches, pears, damson plums. Nobody around—just battered old refrigerators full of fruit, a scales, a money box with about twenty dollars in change and a board across it painted with HONOR SYSTEM.

I took three peaches and paid. I wished Mr. Taraddei had been there. There's a heap down by the creek that I'd lay money is a ruin, but whether Hispanic or Puebloan—or both, one on top of the other—I can't tell.

September

≈

Four a.m.

I write by candlelight. The dim air is thick with ghosts. The small flame rises, sinks. Crickets, a quick, even pulse; some other intermittent nighttime shriller; the soft, knocking rustle of cottonwood leaves. A distant dog.

The neighborhood wakes. A few car engines begin. I can't get too romantic: an ancient truck has just breathed its emphysemic last under my window. Its owner is cussing and slamming. This is not the mystic mountain night.

An ordinance has been passed about keeping dogs penned. A neighbor told me yesterday that Placitas dogs used to hunt in packs and kill livestock. Every so often, in the dead of night, you'd hear a volley of rifle shots, and the dog population would drop for a while.

As I set out this morning to hike I asked Max, who was plastering the driveway wall, if there was a way up to the ridge behind his dad's house. He said there was an easement along the ditch to the Tanque de las Ciruelas, and added, "There are all kinds of roads back there, to the Yellow Mines."

I said, "What are the Yellow Mines?"

Nothing important, he said. Just a bunch of prospects, all they found was iron or something. But *The Yellow Mines*—it sounds like the treasures of Cathay, foreign and golden.

I found the path along the ditch, but it was nearly overgrown and I had to bushwhack, scratching my legs and worrying about rattlers. September-October is when they roam. I scrambled up the embankment to the tanque, which was clear and beautiful. There was a sound of rushing water, but I couldn't pinpoint it. I edged along the east side of the tanque, by the houses—lucky stiffs, to live up there!—and hiked on up.

At the head of the ditch were three big rusty water tanks, Placitas' drinking water. Water gushed from a pipe. Another big pipe went on above and I followed it to a tunnel in the side of the hill. The cinderblock adit was new, but was it originally a mine tunnel?

It was black as the day was bright, and rang with the sound of water. Away back in was a rusty door, behind it water's rush and ring. Across the square blackness of the tunnel's mouth were two perfect orb spider webs, one behind the other. Double-spider-posted: keep out.

I climbed on, to the limestone ridge above the high red road where I walk in the morning. Above the ridge is a wide, level limestone bench where the afternoon sun was warm and glittery, the wind was wide. Two sopilotes came cruising to check me out, coasting so low over my head that I ducked.

At the point of that ridge is a heap of rocks that was once a round structure. I bet it's a lookout that dates from the days of the Navajo raids: from it one can see the whole valley, and though Cerro de Mañana is higher, a lookout here would be closer to the village. Was it once a tower?

A roadrunner puttered calmly along the ridge, flapping its tail.

I hiked back toward the mountains, along the top of the ridge. As it neared Dome Valley the ridge grew a path. Lying next to the path was a pair of huge, rusty scissors, their chrome rusted to bronze.

Scissors?

When I was sure I was in the National Forest I dropped down to the village road. The yellow-green wing of a lesser goldfinch lay in the street like a butterfly wing. Then a big piece of fresh mistletoe, the same greenish-yellow as the wing.

When I got home I asked Max about the round structure. He didn't know what it had been, and said only that in his day it was already down.

Crickets, and a clicking that I think is bats.

The world is too strange.

In the morning, below Tanque del Oso, I met a fat, furry, teddy-bear tarantula ambling along the dirt road. When I nudged it with my sneaker it raised its butt and shot out two pincery things, spinnerets I suppose, since they were in the back. I fetched a stick and frog-marched it off the road and into the ditch. Perhaps tarantulas prefer to walk on a smooth road as much as we do.

Also in the road was a prehistoric flint scraper.

I squatted awhile by a tunnel of those nocturnal ants that curl up and die instantly if touched by bright sun. The morning was early and overcast and a few were still bustling topside, pale as albinos.

Then I drove the freeway to the city. In a parking lot by the university there was a fuss: police flashers, turned heads. A young man lay on his belly, buck naked, manacled hand to foot.

"I'm the acorn!" he yelled. "Fuck Jesus Christ! Fuck Mother Earth!" and so on in that vein. Drug-addled, he had jumped into the Frontier Restaurant's grease-recycling dumpster. The police had nabbed and tied him, though he must have been slicker than a greased piglet.

An ambulance waited. The police turned him over and hosed him down with the Frontier's vegetable mister. "So wash me!" he screamed. "I'm dirt!" The expression of the burly cop who hosed his genitals was shamed, hilarious, secretive, sly. They plunked the screamer face down on a stretcher, still chained, under a pink blanket. The ambulance sped away.

Onlookers stood around exclaiming and describing: re-making their worlds, smoothing over the place where a naked, manacled man had yelled, "I'm the acorn!"

Fuck Mother Earth? Fuck tarantulas and prehistoric scrapers and albino ants?

I think I'll go home to Placitas and take a walk.

The grandmother cottonwood above the grassy field begins to change from the full blackish-green of summer to a paler shade, almost springlike but with yellow beginning in it.

All colors are moist, damp. The road to the tanque is muddy and slippery. A brown sunflower jiggles violently as a seed-seeking jay jumps into the air.

Storm in the small hours. I wore earplugs because of a cricket in the room, and the storm woke me anyway. Roar of wind, rain rattling on the roof—thunder, too, but what woke me was the *roar*. Tossing tree branches, black-and-silver light, that roar—and me safe and dark in old adobe.

I found an arrowhead. It had rained so hard for the last couple of nights that at Tanque del Oso, where the Pueblo ruin was backhoed years ago, many new potsherds had washed out. I tossed them back up on top of the dump, then saw a glittering edge of worked obsidian: a beautiful little point like a razorblade, missing its tip.

Max says he's never found a nicer one. I looked it up: it's a P4, from sometime between 1300 and 1540.

Before sunrise Tanque del Oso was still as a mirror. Pond lilies floated, perfectly round. In the middle swam one mallard drake, talking softly to himself.

As I came home there was a fuss among the chickens. A big hawk flew off at knee-level and stood on the neighbors' roof, looking at me, until I came close and waved my arms.

The chickens are all accounted for, but I don't hope.

Ancestral Traits

Our hens have thighs
like the running dinosaurs from which
they are descended.
Perhaps the Jurassic dusk
was made homely by mutter, chuck,
and throaty croon.

There is still a pair of hummingbirds at the feeder in the chilly dawn. The trees are turning.

The tanque mallard is still swimming by himself, the picture of loneliness. Both yesterday and today I stood on the same bank, at the same spot, as the mallard swam and the sun came over the hill. I felt its warmth on my cheek and saw the edges of everything turn gold.

Enigmas.

One: In this bone-dry weather, worms were crawling across the tarmac of the upper road. All of them were traveling south to north.

Two: Before sunup, on the clean edge of the pavement where the Sandoval County street sweeper had passed so recently that the wet brush marks were still clear, was a little heap of wheat. Perhaps forty grains, perfectly dry. Nothing else like it anywhere, near or far.

Earnest, sandy worms are still crossing the road from south to north.

In the Dome Valley road lay the curlicue mummy of a tiny silver snake. Maybe five inches long, with minuscule scales and a tiny dark eye. Not a garter snake, for it had a blunt tail.

An orb spider's web was strung between chollas: one guyline was seven feet long.

The bird that makes the sudden, loud, rubber-ducky squeak is some kind of nuthatch or woodpecker. Salt-and-pepper body, bright red head.

The bachelor mallard is still quietly paddling in Tanque del Oso.

In the patio a Townsend's warbler sang its one note.

In the patio. I am honored.

Townsend's Solitaire

Where the village meets the trees
and the brown road
leans on the hill,
one
lonely note.

Deep
in the ditchside cottonwood,
the singer, invisible,
has found her
word.

October

As I drove home at dusk on the lower village road I saw the tiny, shiny eye of some small creature in the middle of the pavement. I slowed down, thinking: Rabbit? It was smaller than a rabbit. Just as I reached it, it flew: a chunky little nightjar.

The mallard is gone from the tanque.

There were beetle trails in the dust this morning. The dragging carapace that had drawn one of them was three-quarters of an inch across and heavy, for it pushed up dirt on either side. The legs left oar marks, as if the beetle had rowed through the dust.

Beetle tracks look like zippers.

I finally got an old Placitas USGS 1:100,000 map.

Names:

The ridge where I walked above Camino Los Altos: Cuchilla Lupe, "Lupe's Knife-ridge."

The big ridge on the far side of Las Huertas Creek, above the Montezuma Mine: Crest of Montezuma.

The canyon on the east fork of Las Huertas Creek: Apache Canyon. I still bet it was Comanches who came raiding down there.

The arroyo that comes down behind the village street: Arroyo Suela, "Shoe-Sole Arroyo."

The arroyo that comes down from Tunnel Springs: Arroyo del Ojo del Horno, "Oven Spring Arroyo."

The ridge all down Las Huertas Creek: Cuchilla de Escala, "Ladder Ridge." The ladder they tied the bodies on?

Right Now

I am so glad
to be here in this clear Sunday light!
As the air got colder
I changed to levi's and a shirt,
now I'm drinking a beer
and listening to other people's chickens
screech distantly like rusty hinges.
There's traffic noise,
but it's smaller than the air.
The lilac leaves don't know
that in a week or two
they must fall.

At four in the morning a coyote stood right below in the arroyo and howled. Probably drooling at the chickens through the fence.

First leaves fall from the mulberry. One whole branch is yellow.

In the dust of Dome Valley road, the narrow prints of a raccoon.

The hens, who lay their eggs all over the place, are in the hen-yard under house arrest.

The first good frost. One of the chickens laid an egg out in the middle of the coop and it froze, a little cold golf ball.

Again a coyote chorus in the arroyo, yips and whines. They follow the hidden arroyo-road down out of the mountains.

The juncos are back.

At the tanque the mallard is back, too. Someone is feeding him, because when he saw me he paddled over, climbed out, and walked right up. Green head, orange feet, gray waistcoat of watered silk.

Halloween and Día de los Muertos are coming. AWOL brought a bat to my doormat, a Mexican free-tail or bits thereof: soft charcoal gray, *big* ears, a square, wrinkled snout full of white needle-teeth. I kept one wing: an umbrella with finest struts, a slender-fingered, webby hand.

Mexican free-tails live in caves. This one was probably migrating, weak, and couldn't keep up.

O sorrow! The Road Commission has covered the red, red curve on Camino Los Altos with cement-colored gravel. To live on this earth, looking, is to get your heart broken.

As I came by the goat farm I heard dogs bark, hens in a fuss as the fleeting dark shadow of a coyote slipped under the trees. The chickens had flown up to the roof of the coop.

I tried to hide from the trick-or-treaters, but three bold ones found me anyway. All of them were chubby. Apparently persistence pays off.

November

On Los Altos road, a dead butterfly with steely-iridescent, blue-purple wings. Very small.

Windless woods, deep, and still cold with night. Cottonwood leaves fall one by one: they sound like an animal walking.

The wind blows clouds of silver light across the moon. Yesterday the mulberry was full of leaves; tonight it's a witch-broom bundle against the sky.

How, with so slight a life, do I do the best I can? What needs me?

I left the car at the mailboxes where the Tecolote road joins the Placitas highway. To my surprise, the Tecolote road had been paved. It was odd to walk it on black tarmac, though it did mean less dust in the eyes.

Where the road crosses Las Huertas Creek I dodged down into the creek bed. I'm still intrigued by the hummock right east of there. I went as close as I dared, hugging the fence, but there's so much new building right there—a hundred yards away two men were working in front of a new double-wide. I did poke my head through the fence, but I slid, hung up on the wire, and got a legful of cactus. Instant karma.

Three-strand fences say, "This is a boundary." Four-strands say, "Keep out." This was a four-strand.

I looked more closely at the site above the fork in the road. Some of the smashed china there is eggshell-fine and must have been somebody's treasured teacups. I walked up the pipeline road to the hill crest, above the canyon that drops toward Tecolote.

The wind was sturdy. I sat on a limestone ledge and looked over the valley at the Sandias' mountain shoulder, at Cabezón far off and hazy in the west. The valley was full of moving air. Suddenly: *Cra-a-a!* Eight ravens, shiny black against the blue sky, sailed out over the canyon and circled to check me out.

As I came off the crest and dodged down among the little foothills I spotted a crumb of red pottery, not as big as a dime and black and white on one side. Flaked basalt and basalt cores were scattered about, and more pottery.

I said aloud, "So where's the house?"

I was standing in it. The tumbled outline of two rooms, a little Placitas field house built into the side of a hill and overlooking a valley. I can think of four or five. I'm sure they were built on hillsides in order to save the valley land for corn.

En route to the car I shamelessly stole a flagstone that road construction had torn out of the bank. I tried to walk along carelessly, as though I hauled rock for exercise.

> Outside, coyotes howl.
> I flashed the porch light on and off
> and did not care
> about chickens. I was tired.
>
> Hundreds and thousands and millions
> and billions of everything.
> Hundreds and thousands and millions
> and billions of felt-tip pens,
> ballpoint pens, plastic markers,
> all of them thrown away.

A big spotted tiger salamander lay dead in the road. Dull greeny-black with yellow spots and a yellow collar. Thickset, a heavy, wet weight when I carried it off the pavement. It had rained and snowed in the night—strange weather for an amphibian to be out. Was it hunting worms on the road? I wish I'd seen it alive.

My favorite chicken—Kwili, of the floppy wattles and friendly disposition—has vanished. I heard coyotes in the arroyo last night, no hen fuss, but this morning there are only three chickens in the hutch.

Alas! Black wreaths!

Kwili is back. Where was she?

Rainy wind, a host of flying leaves, spatter at the glass. All night the little feet of rain on the roof.

One last cold, unhappy male mantis. Prodded, he still stirred.

I woke at five to finish a project. The wind howled at the west windows in the dark. Outside all was misted and frosted with snow, cloud-cover lit by the moon that shone somewhere deep within it. Black trees, black mountains; dim, moving mists and moils of snowy wind.

In the middle of the dirt road by Tanque del Oso is the foundation of a house ruin. The roadbed had covered it, but rains have worn away the soil. I noticed it because its rocks were black against a skiff of snow.

At first I assumed it was bedrock, but it makes a perfectly clean right angle of biggish square blocks. Because of their size and regularity it looks early Hispanic rather than Ancestral Puebloan. Next to it is a patch where, months ago, I saw a black smudge in the road and wondered why someone had built a fire there. Now I think it's a midden, fireplace ashes.

In the big field there's a worn and sunken swale that's neither an arroyo nor a draw. Perhaps an old road to the Ojo?

Whoosh! in the headlights, a big owl. No chicken in its clutches.

Hiked down Las Huertas Creek from the end of the Tecolote road to within sight of the freeway. A pale winter day, odd light.

In the creek bed about a mile from the car was a head-sized boulder chock full of horn coral. I carried it home in my arms like a bowling ball. I bet it weighed fifteen pounds, and did I sweat!

Horn coral dates to the Pennsylvanian, the middle of the Carboniferous Period, 250-300 million years ago. Its job for the next few million will be as a doorstop.

I took a sanity walk toward Tecolote and stopped again, irresistibly, to poke around in the fifties dump just off the road. I say fifties, but it may be earlier. I connect it to Tecolote because of its location and because it has so many broken wine bottles and wine glasses; until Prohibition, Tecolote was a wine-growing hacienda.

Among the broken glass were three mother-of-pearl buttons, as beautiful and historic as any jewels. And a hiney: the broken back half of a china doll, stamped JAPAN. I once owned that identical doll, ten cents at the Benjamin Franklin store.

Oddest of all: a small, sunburned cowrie shell.

The tanque mallard came right up and let me touch his cool back, his curly drakestail feathers.

Cold, windy, brilliant sun. Snow *smokes* off the mountain's head in a silver plume—moving so fast, at such a distance, that if someone asked me to judge I'd say, "A hundred miles an hour." Bright silver against the bright blue sky.

A neighbor taught me his father's greeting: "Que Dios le de buen día por no mentar al Diablo"—"May God give you a good day for not mentioning the Devil." I'm not in the habit of mentioning the Devil, but I guess one must take every precaution.

In New Mexico the full, proper greeting is "Buenos días le de Dios"—"May God give you good days." A Northern New Mexican will reprove your ill manners if you greet him as they do in Mexico, simply with, "Buenos días." He'll tell you, "'Buenos días' dice el Diablo por no mentar a Dios"—"The Devil says [only] 'Buenos días' so as not to mention God."

Another morning greeting, sort of like "How are you?" is "Cómo amanació?"—"How were you when you woke?" The proper response is "Muy bien, gracias"—"Very well, thank you." But if you want to be clever you can answer:

"Descalzo y empeloto"—"barefoot and naked."

Or a few less printable dichos.

December

It rained softly all night. I woke to dim drizzle but walked anyway. Light drops prickled my cheeks, as though I walked through the cloud itself. I had turned back home, my face into the cloud, when suddenly: a breath: a roar: a wind surged up the valley and in a twinkling blew the whole cloud away. Air full of leaves and birds, sun fitfully winking, sky purple and the mountain flank bright yellow.

Yowza!

Cabezón

Jemez Storm

I watched the storm come in
from Jemez, blowing in front of it
dust, birds, rain,
as though the birds
drew the rain.

Wind whistles.
I think it is not
wind, but the world
whirling away from the sun
inside its jacket of air.

Gazing down-valley
at the Rio Grande—its gravels tracked
by eons of human travel—
is like sitting on a shaded porch,
watching the road.

Something big came rushing up-valley
and threw rain at me.

Last night somebody's chicken bit the dust on the high red road:
feathers in two big piles with a languid dribble between. Black
feathers, now edged with frost.
    Not our chicken.

There's a place on the high road from which you can see four sacred
mountains. Redondo, patchy with snow; Cabezón, a dark tooth;
Mount Taylor, all white; and the shoulder of Sandia Crest, Ocupiñ.
    Next to the house foundation in the road by the tanque,
near where I found the obsidian point, there's a jumble of rocks

weathering out of the roadcut. The rock jumble—part of it a squared corner—is on a level with the foundation. Many potsherds.

Thinking about the circular ruin on the north end of Cerro Negro, the petroglyph ridge. Is it, like the stone ring on the ridge above the DeLaras', perhaps a lookout? Both overlook Las Huertas Creek, the way the Navajo raiders came.

But the Apaches (Comanches! Comanches!) came down Apache Canyon. Did the settlers have to look two ways at once?

Winter Solstice

A little snow scours the ground.
Pale, directionless light
blunders around the morning.
The sun stands still.
We settle in
to feel our way to spring.

January

Hiked the hills east of San Francisco Road with a friend. Dogs came out and barked until we disappeared. Three hours of gully-hopping, enhanced by one smashed purple wine bottle and one beautiful seedpod, don't know of what but it rattles. The wind was cold, a knife. Shadows crept out from the ridge, and we came back in the rising dark.

To record: standing on the east side of that ridge, looking east, still a slight afterglow on the ragged desert plain, the snowy Ortiz rising above the mesas and the Sangre de Cristo range white, bluing down. Two tiny, distant lights, almost to Santa Fe. To the west, Cabezón a gunsight on the orange horizon, the tilted flat mesas stepping down above the river. Behind us, dogs barking, invisible among invisible junked cars.

Huge country. Huge. Glad I got to see it before it fills up.

Ground sodden with melted snow, ice on the mud puddles. As I came down from the tanque this morning, dogs kicked up a fuss and, right front of me, a coyote crossed the road. Then another. Then a third, big, yellow-gray, bushy with winter.

They glanced at me but didn't break stride. All three belonged entirely to themselves.

A fat winter roadrunner is making the rounds of the patio.
Looking for what? They're carnivorous. Snow lizards?

Oh no—too early, daffodil snouts!

Year Four

February

As I walked the road by the mission church two juncos flew round a corner, close to the ground, and practically ran into me. They burst straight up from my ankles and past my face—a flash of white feathers in front of my eyes.

Last night, wired from deadlines and miserable with allergy, I dreamed I was in a big house that was slowly being taken over by ghosts like Navajo chindi. They weren't humanlike but rather "bad patches," malevolent or anti-life, that moved around like heat-ripples or changed qualities in the air. I saw one coming, could not avoid it, so instead I threw myself into it with a shout that was part terror and part the karate-chop that says, "*I am!*"

With that yell I woke myself up. Today I have a sore throat.

March

The daffodils are open.

"The airfolk at their courting," Kenneth Patchen says: this morning I watched a robin dance. On a branch in front of the female, the male strutted back and forth—and incidentally seemed nearly to slip off a few times. He raised his head feathers in a little crest, and sometimes kept his beak open. Look at me!

In spite of the drought there are birds all over. Spring songs.

March Drought

Wind whines at the saltbush,
a mockingbird scrambles phrases in the elm.
A white spring, many fires.
Under the tin eaves
the steadfast phoebe sits her nest.

April

First hummingbird. They've been here for two and a half weeks, in spite of frost and snow, but I was away teaching in Zuni and have only now put out their tipple.

In the late dusk, shapes have gone to silhouettes against the still-pale sky. Moths flutter in to sip at the lilacs. Orion sets low over the western horizon, ready to disappear for summer. The dipper points to the north star.

Our lives are so brief.

Evening

The low gold sun
lights insect wings
in thousands,
a second village
hovering in air
above the human one.
The snarl
of a chain saw, distant,
is the same voice
as a fly's.

Standing in the road with a neighbor and looking at a Jerusalem cricket, so-called "child of the earth" or "earth baby":

Neighbor: Oh god, it looks like a little alien. An extraterrestrial fetus.

Me: I think it looks like a kid in a stripy tee shirt.

Neighbor: How benign. You're perverse, but benign.

May

Wind in the salt cedar, the poplars, the cottonwoods.

In Placitas in summer I see far more hummingbirds than flies.

The most suspended and pristine of New Mexico mornings. I'm still full of yesterday's long, scrambly hike in the Jemez: hush of wind in ponderosa, dusty, glittery, sandy cliffs.

Only this one life I've got. How shall I spend it?

> What happens is
> sometimes I forget
> that where I-40
> does its Roman cut-and-fill
> across the world
> there's an animal track
> that turns left.
> I forget
> the fanged one,
> the towhee, the dirt,
> the day. And it is all
> always
> there.

Oh dear. One of our two ducks has vanished. At 4:30 this morning I heard duck-mutter, the preoccupied, worried kind. I thought nothing of it except to feel annoyed to be waked at 4:30. Now we are one duck short. I don't know that this poultry experiment will be successful.

The air is crystalline, washed, the patio checkered with light and shade. Hummingbirds squeak at both feeders. The scarlet poppies are enormous, the biggest I've ever seen.

Soon summer?

June

Stipa seedheads shining silver in the morning wind. A warbler shot over me, its breast so yellow it looked orange. As always I am in awe: stunned, paying attention, smelling damp sand and the odor of dark, looking out for birds and bears and tiny, angry rattlesnakes.

It is all right to dwell in this awe, in geologic time and the millennial power of rainwater.

Be still. Listen.

Last night there was a soft ruckus on the roof gravel that went on and on. Something the weight of a large cat was rustling and scrabbling up there—not trotting about but staying in one place.

My first guess was that it was an owl, eating the remaining duck. The second was that it was the War Twins, playing stickball on the roof because I hadn't given them a food offering when I was hiking in their wilderness.

I got up and slammed the door a couple of times. The noise quit. Just quit; it didn't trot off, so it must have been a large bird. I'm glad it went away. It was a dark night and I would have felt weird, barefoot in my sleep shirt, lobbing rocks up there at something I couldn't see.

This morning I watched a coyote make off across a stubble field with somebody's russet chicken in its mouth.

An artist friend said, "I feel like I'm irresponsible sometimes, but I'm just going ahead and living."

Scutter and scold in the saltbush: scaled quail. The cholla are downtrodden and purple with drought. I've been dumping water on the worst-looking. The biggest looks all right; it even has yellow fruit.

   With the first heavy rains the erosion will be terrible.

The ruins of Ojo de la Casa. As many times as I've clambered around that area I never knew they were there. I was always farther downstream.

   They're like the ruins of a tiny Italian hill town, houses clustered on a rocky outcrop. The shards of glass around the highest house were very old—oxidized green bottles with thick lips. Deep purple manganese glass, which means they were made before 1914.

The neighbor's five-year-old stuck his head in my window this morning to announce he was looking for the hens' eggs and couldn't find them. Did I know where they were? I said I didn't. He turned to our duck and said, "Do *you* know where those nesteses are?"

I stood a long time on Camino Los Altos watching a fat bumblebee in a forest of sweet pea: prying, fumbling, poking and nuzzling the pinky-purple flowers. Now and then it stopped to rub the pollen off its face and head like a cat. Big old buzzy thing. I'll take the bumblebee as my insect totem, so fumbly and persistent.

   There was a whirling swarm of birds, but it wasn't birds. A little dust devil had gotten into the roadside tumbleweeds, shredded them and blown them into the air. Like birds they hopped up and sailed down.

Summer Solstice

On the longest day of the year,
walking
in the shortest shade.

Such a late spring. It's almost July, and the apricots aren't ripe.

By Ojo del Oso the stipa seeds are drilling themselves into cracks in the ground. It's as though they could sense the broken places and grope over to them.

A shiny black perrodo stumps across the road.

A hike down the Ojo del Horno arroyo is very green, in and out of sulfur-smelling water. Willows, matriarchal cottonwoods. At the confluence with Tunnel Springs arroyo there's a stand of cattails.

I followed the arroyo—now and then clambering out to see where I was—to the petroglyph ridge, and climbed it. These are petroglyphs that I haven't seen printed anywhere, though I'm sure they've been recorded. One looks like a menstruating woman, though the blood droplets are clearly more recent than the figure itself. Maybe a hippie joke postscript?

I went looking for them because I'd been to a lecture by a petroglyph expert who described one of them, which looks like a horned toad licking the sun, as a "lizard-person." However, said expert was so obnoxiously academic and jargony that I was really put off.

There was a little heap-of-stones fieldhouse site at the base of the ridge, right next to the arroyo, and a large potsherd of sloppy late polychrome, red and black on cream.

This morning I thought to walk down the arroyo from 165, but the bottom is too densely wooded with huge cottonwoods and willows and other small growth. Instead I billygoated along the rim, skirted crumbling cliffs and undercuts and dodged up and down side-arroyos. It feels secret down there, as under heavy trees and plant growth: green, dark, impassable, down out of the wind. As though there were a private life in progress.

There is. It has to do with water. In the far bank, hidden by leaves, was a loud silver tinkle: a spring in the soft alluvium, like the one in Arroyo del Ojo del Horno.

More even than most Placitas arroyos, this one has a feeling of belonging only to itself. Perhaps also to animals and children? A non-Hispanic, rather New Age neighbor told me the arroyo had been used by curanderas for their rites. That it was sweet and benevolent.

It didn't feel any sweet and benevolent to me. It felt Other. Arroyos always do.

The arroyo to the east—Arroyo del Ojo del Horno—is *beautiful*. Totally different in character: waterless, with a wide, light bottom of coarse sand. It's full of trees, so water must flow underground, but there's little underbrush. Here and there the sandstone bedrock is exposed. It has a benign, clean, open feel—Southern Utah, Grand Gulch—compared to the dark, wet secrecy of the arroyo to the west.

Many footprints of dogs or coyotes. What a lovely place.

A neighbor says two months ago he found a mountain lion's footprints in that arroyo.

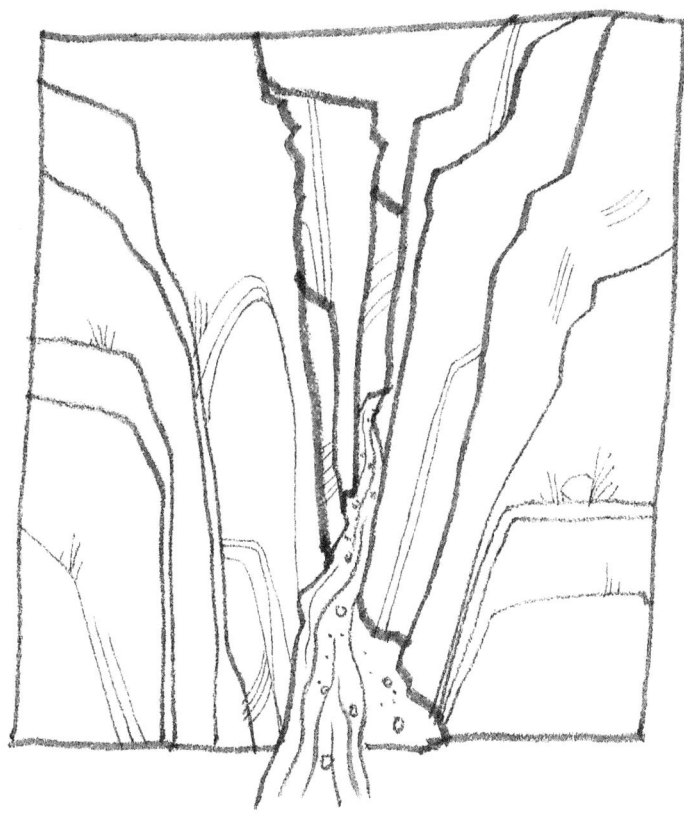

Things Found in the Road:

A white eggshell, quail size.

A yin-yang pendant, run over and the worse for wear.

Sowbug tracks in the fine dust. They look like tractor tracks.

Roadkill: crickets, beetles, sowbugs, centipedes, children of the earth. Salamanders. A strange native bee, russet orange. The road is a dangerous environment.

A big roadkill bull snake. Someone took it up and wove it in and out of a hogwire fence. It hung there a while, sagging in strange dried loops, the flesh picked out by birds.

In the middle of the road, one solitary, fresh, green jalapeño pepper. What the hell?

More roadkill. In front of the church this morning another bull snake, maybe eighteen inches long. It lay in a perfect circle like the Benzene Ring snake, as if it were eating its tail:

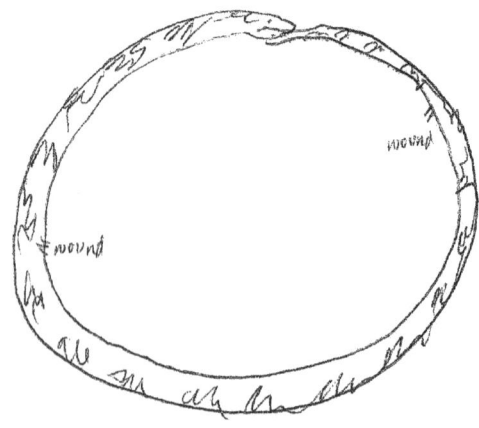

I picked it up—it was limp and cool—and laid it behind a wall.

Snake Shedding

Skin dry and too tight,
eyes cloudy,
the snake lies in the May sun.

It is in vision that the change begins:
a fine line
creeps through the center of the world,
a crack that can widen.

She convulses.
The thin, dry membrane splits,
pulls back from the cornea
and curls away, unzipping
down the length of the back.

When the new, soft serpent
coils out in her painted hide,
her eyes are clear.

In another age I think I might have been an ecstatic, a dancer.

July

First monsoon rain.

The overpowering honey of wet grass. Bird chirp.

Again. One of the chicks guaranteed to be a hen has had a sex change. S/he roosts in the tree outside my bedroom window and crows at will, usually between two and four a.m. I'd deport her to the coyotes but I'm feeling bad about all the roadkill.

They say roosters crow at sunrise, but in reality roosters crow whenever. Law of averages says now and then a sunrise will coincide.

I woke to steady rain and the rich melancholy I associate with the damp east. Spicy and bleak.

More roadkill. Sad but funny: a large mouse, in the cartoon classic stopped-in-its-tracks pose:

Nocturnal, for it had perfectly enormous ears.

This morning I set out jaded. Restored by walking, though still inclined toward this awareness of roadkill. Painful to look at was a black beetle, its abdomen in rags and its eggs hanging out splattered. It had happened long enough ago for the wound to dry, yet the beetle had dragged itself off the road and was still patiently trying to arrange its legs to do something, perhaps climb the bank. As if it were still dutifully on its autonomic nervous system but its reasoning, such as it had, was beginning to wind down. I watched it in horror and awe for a moment, then squashed it with a rock. Afterward I wondered whether I should have, it seemed so honestly its own being.

Two more: a stripy lizard right in front of our house, and a little horned toad squashed into an Ernest Shepard ink drawing of dancing Mr. Toad. Funny. Grim.

Trumpet vine: how they open. First there's the sturdy orange tube, its package of petals tight shut. Then the petals untuck like the flaps of a box.

Above the abandoned vineyard by the Dome Valley road, over the ridge from the old malachite working, is a scatter of stones that may well be a field house. There's a concentration of flakes and potsherds. As many times as I've walked across that field, how have I not noticed this?

By the vineyard field a coyote dodged out of the bushes. Thin, angular, nervous, he looked back at me repeatedly, a kind of stiffness in his trot.

Summer walks on. The last apricots fall, flattened and drying on the roads ... roadkill apricots! The buffalo gourds grow fat and dark green.

There's a hummingbird nest on the patio and the mama bird is setting, very alert. In the mulberry is a sloppy sparrow construction, dad sparrow in attendance.

Roadkill Awareness Month continues. Good heavens. This time it was a female robin with her speckled breast. Little and cool, with limp feet. I put her body over the fence into the field.

Jack

I found a jackrabbit dead
at the road's edge—
legs crooked,
ears flat, eyes dull.
So still.
This soul that we
are supposed to have, and they
are supposed to lack—
I think it must be
not our personhood, not
what each one of us owns, but
the shine given off
by a trillion beings working
in almost-harmony:
the colony we are,
our home.
This rabbit, stopped
at the road's edge,
seems so finally dead
because here a trillion beings
are dead.
This was once
a nation.

Is there more and more traffic in Placitas, to account for these squashed animals? This morning it was a centipede, the fat, six-inch kind. As with the black beetle, its rear half had been run over and pasted to the road but the front half still feebly reacted. The ants were already at it; it twisted its body flinchingly this way and that. I did not play God this time as I had with the beetle, I don't know why. Because it was gruesomely a centipede? Yet I felt as sorry for it, pestered by ants.

When I came back down the road ten minutes later it was finishing its dying, and hardly reacted at all.

The goddamned hen-turned-rooster crowed again in the wee smalls. This time I didn't debate. I got up, stuffed my nightshirt into my shorts, climbed the tamarisk and grabbed that guy—terrible shrieks—revved up the truck, drove to the edge of civilization, and chucked him out the window, saying, "Out you go and pedal your bike." Drove home and went back to bed.

Hecho. Or for the coyotes: Buen provecho.

August

Summer in her fatness.

Fat yucca pods. Fat orange of the last apricots and the pears. I picked up a handful of tiny, twinned, fat green acorns.

Ran into a man on the Dome Valley road who talked about a development going in up there: twenty-seven wells.

On Camino Los Altos was a rufous hummingbird. Squeaking, it scuttered along the ground like a Flit-bombed fly. I carried it home in my hand, a live coal. It's in a covered bucket now, waiting for me to take it to Animal Rescue.

I just realized why scaled quail have that goofy blond topknot: it blends perfectly with a field of dry desert grass.

By the tanque, in the finer-than-talcum dust by the house-construction site, are the tank-tread trails of about a hundred beetles. Every one bears northeast-southwest. Why?

Also in the dust, lower down, the fat paddy-paws of a Dome Valley raccoon.

I went through the checkout at the market behind a dignified, fat, black-haired Pueblo grandma in a cloud-terrace hairdo with a chongo, a red-and-orange floral homemade dress, and moccasins. A careful shopper, she was buying only the loss leaders: sacks and sacks of flour, twenty-five pounds for two-fifty; macaroni dinners, twenty or so; sugar; salt. They left in the granddaughter's up-to-the-minute, four-wheel drive SUV.

At the junction of Camino Los Altos with the village street is a handsome new house with a very, *very* shiny tin roof.

Heat. Stillness. Drought. The Sahel just around the corner.
    A scrub jay in the Gambel oak was yanking off green acorns and whacking them on a branch. It did not care that I was four feet away.

August Drought

Stalled on the highest
Ferris-wheel curve of summer,
swinging slightly,
the year hangs in heat.
So dry.
So still.
Even the swinging
stops.

Come *down!*
Come *down!* we cry.
Fall rain, come dark,
break
this long high note.
We promise never again
to beg for light.

The sun burns
in the white sky.

In the street by the stop sign I found the much-mauled wing of a large raptor, torn off at the shoulder. Perhaps, from its softness, an owl.

Big Bang

The hard part:
letting go
of what you never finished,
what
you never began.
Don't cry.
The whole
universe is a sigh.

Rain. The sweet smell of cedar blows over the mountain.

Again rain. We are thankful.

A friend tells me he showed a horned toad to his granddaughter, who is two. She held out her hands for it and cried, "Einosaur!"

September

Right in the middle of the village street there's a pile of bear scat full of apricot pits. Where are the bears finding apricots in September? Maybe they're plum pits?

Harvest

Right before sunrise
a bear came down the ditch,
climbed the pear tree
and broke a branch,
crossed the road,
crashed the fence,
ate the tomatoes,
squashed the cantaloupes
and left.
Nothing there now
but a big drippy dropping
full of peach pits.

On my walk I chatted with a neighbor woman, born in Placitas. As we passed the church she absent-mindedly, and without a break in the conversation, crossed herself: a beautiful, unconscious gesture.

First yellow leaf on the mulberry.

Today I learned that I must leave this house by Christmas.

This morning I was surrounded by a circle of singing coyotes: close above Camino Los Altos, on the ridge behind the village, and from the foot of Cerro de Mañana.

It occurs to me that the stone used to build the embankment of Tanque del Oso probably came from the house ruins whose outlines are visible in the dirt road.

A pile of chicken feathers outside the blue gate. I came to the obvious conclusion, but all chickens were accounted for so I forgot about it. Then I noticed that Hysteria Hen, the red one who goes outside the gate to lay, has a bare rump: only one long feather left.

Winter with a cold butt.

When I see our duck, Sir Francis Drake, so happy and duckish in nothing but an irrigation ditch that's exactly as wide as he is, I say, "*Deo gratias.*"

I woke to cold and wind. Pre-dawn was delicious, me snuggled in the comforter in the dark with a cold nose, listening to the wind in the cottonwood. This will yellow the leaves.

October

Last night a little gray fox fled across the road in my headlights. Low-built, tail nearly as big as its body.

A neighbor came to tell me a bear was seen ambling on Camino Los Altos, and I should be careful on my morning walk.

No Credit

We have not so much
learned as happened,
the way grass springs up
where the bear shat.

I overslept and had nightmares so I hiked up Tunnel Springs trail.

Spiders had spun their webs across it. All alone in the sky, a raven harried a hawk. Then there were two more hawks cruising south over the mountain shoulder, more ravens prodding them, all of them in a swirl over the round peak. They shrank to smaller, more distant specks, until the ravens came back alone.

Sandia Limestone

I found a ledge for lunch.
The dirty city crawled and hooted
far below, but where I sat
had been another town,
the stem-and-shell
neighborhood of some old sea.
A sunny place,
now as then; the wind cut cold
but the stone was warm.
I swung my feet,
ate grapes and spit
the seeds into the abyss.
Who will sit,
someday, on what's left of us?
Will warm rears
thank us,
in six hundred million years?

The way I get to Tanque del Oso has been to climb over the fallen
fence and walk through the willows to the pond. Just this morning—
almost on the eve of leaving Placitas—I saw that there is an entrance
built into the fence. Whoever fenced the tanque wrapped the wire
separately around the two trunks of a split juniper:

The barbed wires have bitten cruelly into the tree.

I stepped through. It felt like a passage, a magic door. Indeed, right in front of it, outside, someone had placed a sandy flagstone as threshold.

Duration

We must learn duration,
as the root
of the creosote bush,
the bristlecone pine,
endure in earth.

Every inch of the road.
Feet bare.

The last, lone hen—Sir Francis and the other two hens vanished last week—mourns throatily in the coop, penned in a space too small for her roaming habits.

The mallard is gone from the tanque. I hope he has flown.

I hiked up Las Huertas Creek from the Tecolote road, nervous about dogs because the houses are built so close now, but in a quarter mile there are no houses.

There's a ruin that looks recent. A third of the walls and three-quarters of the roof are down, the vigas tipped into the empty rooms. A beautiful, peaceful place with no building for acres all around, a long view down the valley, the multilayered hills. Not much purple glass, so I'll bet the place dates from the twenties or thirties. Below the ruin was a clump of iris. A couple of years ago I'd seen it in bloom. I found a piece of junk aluminum in the creek and used it to dig up nine corms to plant when I have a home again.

In New Mexican Spanish iris are lirios, lilies.

I came home cross-country. Someone has plowed a road up to the top of Cerro de Mañana, preparing to build a house. I didn't look for the shrine.

November

It rained last night. The birds sing frail rain songs, as if it were spring.

This morning, in the dust of the road, the long, soft marks left by the back legs of a sitting rabbit.

I led a bunch of first graders in writing a story.

Me: Okay, so the farmer has a nice, big, fat pig! What could happen next?

Child in front row: Una matanza!

The leaves of the buffalo gourds have collapsed. A frost.

The wind-sound of the cottonwood is louder in winter than in summer, because the leaves dry but don't fall.

Breathing Stone

It took the winter sparrows
two days to understand
they were being fed.
They will never understand
it is I who feed them.

Great steppes of space.
On them a tiny figure trudges,
distant, dark, right
as a winter marmot
on a snowfield:
myself,
walking on.

This is my forty-ninth
year of breath.
The wind smells of wet stone:
that means
I suck in, breathe out particles of stone
too small to see.
I am breathing stone.

This morning, walking, I spotted one pretty white chert flake, its bulb of percussion very clear, embedded in the tarmac of Placitas Heights. Perhaps it had been part of the surface gravel?

Early morning. The wild squealing of a pig from among the clustered old houses: una matanza, a butchering for Christmas tamales.

Windy, cold. Last night the dank wind pushed a cowl of cloud over Sandia Crest and raked it down the east front, a dragon creeping east over the pinnacles. I stopped the truck at the S-curves to watch it creep.

As I walked up Dome Valley road, a gust filled the air with cottonwood leaves like a migration of starlings.

Day after Thanksgiving.

I took my grandfather's ornate end nippers up the village street to the split gateway juniper below Tanque del Oso and cut away the barbed wire that was strangling the tree.

Other than a thousand times trespassing, I have done very few illegal things in my life. This one pleased me very much.

Old Juniper

Some branches gray,
my heart still sappy.
Brief lives
through my branches
flirt and trill.
In this stone place
my roots find water.
Bless my back,
white sun!

ENVOI

Morning Mockingbird

Thanks and praise.
What are "thanks and praise"
from a cluster of nuclei,
a colony of clever bacteria,
a mortal mammal
whose task is to continue
for no reason it can know?
(A trillion trillion suns.)
Thanks and praise!
That the morning is cool.
That your back against my breast is warm.
That there is food.
That the mockingbird invents order,
repeats it,
throws it away.

Acknowledgments

I would like to thank the Placiteños: descendants of First Peoples, later settlers and incomers, hippies and suburbanites alike. Special gratitude goes to the late Max DeLara for many good conversations. I am indebted to many for reminders and suggestions as a journal became a book—especially to Bernalillo's historian, Martha Liebert, for recognizing that gossip and history belong to each other and need to be gently sorted.

Most of all I'm grateful to and for the creatures of Placitas—the coyotes, owls and salamanders, ravens and nighthawks, moths and worms and ducks and dogs—who kept me reminded of our shared mortality. I was privileged, for a little while, to be one of them.

This book is not a history but a record, and all the errors in it are mine.

References and Suggested Reading

Bernalillo: Between the River and a Hard Place. Martha Liebert. University of New Mexico Press, 2021.

Captives and Cousins: Slavery, Kinship, and Community in the Southwest Borderlands. James F. Brooks. University of South Carolina Press, 2002.

Las Placitas: Historical Facts and Legends. Lou Sage Batchen. Tumbleweed Press, 1972.

Pláticas del Pasado: Conversations of the Past. Illustrated by Vivian DeLara. Tumbleweed Press, 1976.

Wild Plants of the Pueblo Province. William W. Dunmire and Gail D. Tierney. Museum of New Mexico Press, 1995.

Village history: lasacequiasdeplacitas.com/historic-village-placitas

Archaeology: San José de las Huertas: galisteo.nmarchaeology.org/sites/san-jose-de-las-huertas.html

Betsy James is the author-illustrator of seventeen books. Her latest novel, *Roadsouls*, was a finalist for the World Fantasy Award. A watercolorist, she is represented by Nedra Matteucci Galleries, Santa Fe. She leads writers' workshops in the University of New Mexico Honors College and lives in Albuquerque's North Valley. Learn more at www.betsyjames.com.

Casa Urraca Press publishes creative nonfiction, poetry, photography, and other works by authors we believe in. New Mexico and the US Southwest are rich in creative and literary talent, and the rest of the world deserves to experience our perspectives. So we champion books that belong in the conversation—books with the power, compassion, and variety to bring very different people closer together.

We are proudly centered in the high desert somewhere near Abiquiú, New Mexico. Our books are available through independent booksellers everywhere. You can visit us online at casaurracapress.com for exquisite editions of our books and to register for workshops with our authors.